Achieving QTS

Assessment for **Learning** and **Teaching**
in Secondary Schools

Martin Fautley
Jonathan Savage

LearningMatters

First published in 2008 by Learning Matters Ltd.
Reprinted in 2008.

British Library Cataloguing in Publication Data
A CIP record for this book is available from the British Library.

ISBN: 978 1 84445 107 4

Cover design by Topics – The Creative Partnership
Text design by Code 5 Design Associates Ltd
Project management by Deer Park Productions, Tavistock
Typeset by PDQ Typesetting Ltd, Newcastle under Lyme
Printed and bound in Great Britain by Bell & Bain Ltd, Glasgow

Learning Matters
33 Southernhay East
Exeter EX1 1NX
Tel: 01392 215560
info@learningmatters.co.uk
www.learningmatters.co.uk

Contents

The Authors

Dr Martin Fautley is a Reader in Education at Birmingham City University. For many years he was a school teacher in the Midlands before undertaking doctoral research at the University of Cambridge.

Dr Jonathan Savage is a Senior Lecturer in Education at the Institute of Education, Manchester Metropolitan University. Until 2001 he was Head of Music at Debenham High School, an 11–16 comprehensive school in rural Suffolk. He is also Managing Director of UCan.tv, a not-for-profit company that produces engaging educational software.

Introduction

The structure of this book

This book is intended to help you in dealing with assessment issues during your time as a trainee teacher, into your first year as a newly qualified teacher, and beyond. It is envisaged that you are currently at a stage where you are thinking about a number of new concepts and terminologies, and are beginning to get to grips with the complex world of the class-room and school (we use the term 'classroom' throughout this book as a shorthand term for any location where teaching and learning take place, be it laboratory, theatre, studio, gymna-sium, gallery, playing field, or any of a myriad of other places).

Thinking about you, the upper part of Figure 1 represents a likely snapshot of you at your current stage of development. This includes your own subject knowledge and knowledge about a range of professional educational issues. This may include some initial exploratory work about assessment types or strategies within your subject area or in the wider context of professional studies.

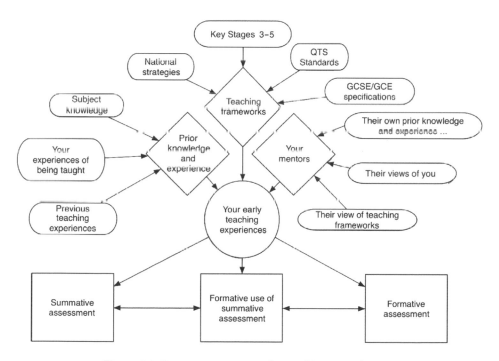

Figure 1 Influences on your early teaching experiences

What Figure 1 shows is that a variety of influences will have had an effect on you, and will continue to do so during your early teaching experiences. No one comes to teaching as a 'blank slate', you will have had a number of experiences – some good, some maybe not so good – which will affect both what and how you think about a number of issues. This prior knowledge you bring with you will obviously vary from one person to another. So, in Chapter 1 you will undertake a basic audit of your knowledge about assessment, its purposes and practices, and will challenge your thinking about what assessment is, and what it involves. This is all focused on the Chapter title, 'Why assess?'

Following this, Chapters 2–4 deal with a number of important issues and concepts regarding assessment. Chapter 2 deals with theoretical approaches to assessment, and discusses how assessment fits in to a learning theory view of processes. Chapters 3 and 4 introduce and discuss the key terminologies of summative and formative assessment, and offer you opportunities to reflect on how these are employed in your day-to-day teaching. We will emphasise the importance of formative assessment throughout this book, and there will be aspects of all these chapters that we hope will again challenge your preconceptions and take your learning forwards with regard to these important areas of educational thought and

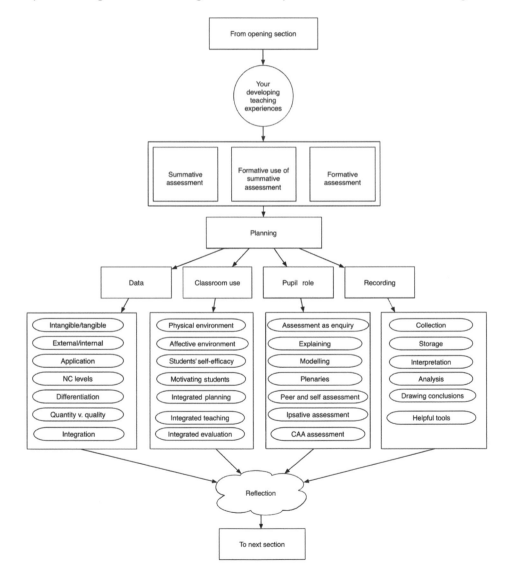

Figure 2 Your developing experiences

practice. The lower part of Figure 1 represents an outline of these chapters, and links directly to Figure 2.

Figure 2 shows linkages from the opening section of this book, where, following these opening chapters, we then turn in Chapters 5–9 to extend the themes we have discussed by both applying and exploring them within a number of contexts. These will include how assessment affects:

- **your planning (Chapter 5);**
- **your understanding of students' ability when measured against various internal and external criteria (Chapter 6);**
- **your classroom practice and how the classroom environment, in its widest sense, can affect this work (Chapter 7);**
- **the student's role within assessment (Chapter 8);**
- **the ways in which you can interpret, analyse and record the outcomes of assessment (Chapter 9).**

Finally, in Chapter 10 we will consider how your work in assessment can be applied and extended within your NQT year. An important part of this work will be based upon your understanding of reflective cycles and how they can be used to underpin your development as a teacher, as illustrated in Figure 3.

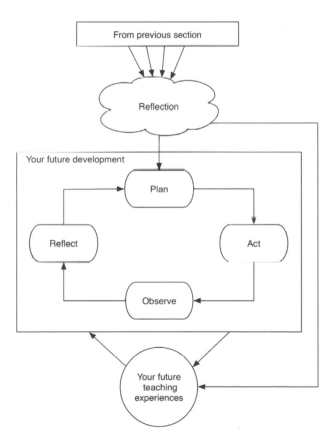

Figure 3 Reflection

1
Why assess?

Introduction

Good assessment practice is a key feature of effective teaching and learning in schools. This seemingly obvious statement hides a wealth of meanings, subtexts, historical arguments, and views of teaching and learning that may seem bewildering to you situated as you are in the early stages of your teaching career. And yet, on a day-to-day basis, teachers and students are assessing in a multitude of different ways, and building different meanings into these assessment processes. This book will examine these issues, discuss problems, ask you to think and reflect on things you have seen and things you do, and work with you on developing your own abilities and competences in using and interpreting assessment in all its multifaceted dimensions as it appears in schools.

We will begin by considering the foundation for assessment, and ask what it is for, what it does, and what happens to the results of it. Let us start by asking you to think about this.

REFLECTIVE TASK

How would you articulate your own personal philosophy (or view) of assessment? Here are some questions to prompt your thinking:

What is assessment?
What is it used for?
What results from assessment?
Who has this information?

Try to jot down a few ideas or sentences that encapsulate these issues.

Spend a few minutes analysing your response: Did you write about formal examinations, such as GCSE or A level? Maybe you wrote about finding out what students know, or about whether they could do things? Perhaps you wrote about giving the students a test, or about checking their work? You might have written about recording marks they had achieved in an assignment, and you might have written about how you would enter these into your mark book. You may have written about having a conversation with the students to discover what they felt about something, or about what they thought about their learning. It is entirely likely that there will be as many different responses to this task as there are readers of this book, which itself tells us that assessment is a complex issue, and not amenable to simple and straightforward responses.

Our starting point for a philosophy of assessment is that it is inextricably bound up with a wider view of teaching and learning, and the answers you gave to the reflective task above will reveal elements of your own view. It is quite likely that as you move through the initial teacher education and training process, and the variety of teaching experiences it contains, your views will change. So, let us now try to unpick some views of teaching and learning and see where and how assessment fits into them.

Assessment and instruction

Historically, assessment was viewed as the thing which happened after learning had taken place. Graue writes how '...assessment and instruction are often conceived as curiously separate in both time and purpose' (Graue, 1993, p291). In this view, a course of 'instruction' is followed by assessment, as shown in Figure 1.1.

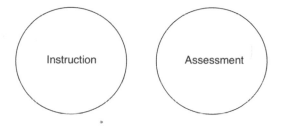

Figure 1.1 'Curiously separate'

If your answer to the reflective task described an examination of the GCSE or A level type, then Figure 1.1 fits this model well. It also applies to instances where the teacher teaches a unit of work, and then gives the students a test at the end to see how much they have learned, or what they scored. This view of teaching and learning often envisions the educative process as comprising blocks of teaching followed by an examination or test of some sort. This way of thinking about teaching, learning and assessment is represented diagrammatically in Figure 1.2.

Teaching	Test	Teaching	Test	Teaching	Test

Figure 1.2 The end-of-unit test model

This way of working was typical of education systems in many countries until relatively recently, and is an example of summative assessment, a key assessment terminology, which we look at in more detail in Chapter 3. An important aspect of summative assessment is that it separates the teaching process from assessment.

> **REFLECTIVE TASK**
>
> In the end-of-unit test model, as shown in Figure 1.2, what do you think it might be that is being tested?

Here it is fairly safe to assume that responses to this reflective task will relate to 'what I taught them in the unit of work', and are likely be variants of two key educational notions – knowledge and skills. Let us deconstruct this a little further.

> **REFLECTIVE TASK**
>
> If knowledge and skills are being tested for in the end-of-unit test model, what is knowledge, and what are skills?

This is much harder to answer. Knowledge is often held to be things which we know, and, as Ryle reminds us (Ryle, 1949), can be divided into 'knowing how' – things which we know how to do practically (e.g. how to change a light-bulb, how to play the piano) – and 'knowing that' – things we know as facts (e.g. the capital of France, or what Ohm's law is). But in a school context, knowledge is accorded varying degrees of status, as Young (1971, 1999) pointed out:

> *The high value of some knowledge is institutionalised by the creation of schools, colleges and universities to transmit it as the curriculum.*
>
> (Young, 1999, p62)

So it is high-status knowledge to know about Ohm's law, but low-status knowledge to know, for instance, how Spider Man got his powers; the former can be investigated in an end-of-unit test, the latter is likely to be dismissed as trivial.

In the case of skills, Ryle's notion of 'knowing how' is leading us towards what skills are, where they are either practically based, or involve mental skills. Thus knowing how to kick a football is a skill, and knowing how to do long division is a skill. Both involve 'knowing how' to accomplish the task. Indeed, it may well be that it is the evidencing of the skill, as in 'show your working', that you as a teacher might deem more important than getting the answer right.

This takes us into another area of assessment, that of evaluation. As custodians of knowledge, it is the teachers, often acting in accordance with externally imposed examination specifications, who will decide what status should be accorded to different types of knowledge. In your classroom you will decide what it is that you teach by deciding what activities, knowledge, skills and concepts you will include in your lesson plans. At the same time as including things in your content, you will be excluding things from it. You will have made an evaluation of what it is that needs to be included, and what you will not be teaching. Evaluation – placing value on things – is an undercurrent in the debate about the philosophy of assessment, and is a contested arena in education.

> **REFLECTIVE TASK**
>
> Think of your own subject area. What would be considered 'high-status' knowledge. and what would not?

In deciding areas of study which you deem important, and therefore placing value upon some areas and not others, it is also appropriate to think about what the students might think about this. We need to acknowledge that students have a wide range of knowledge, skills and understanding which they bring with them to any learning situation. The personalisation of learning, which we deal with in detail in Chapter 8, means that you should be aware of the students' values too.

REFLECTIVE TASK

Next time you introduce a new topic, and explain what it is that the students will be learning, in other words what is valued knowledge, why not also try asking them what they know of this topic already, what they think is important in it, and what aspects of it they feel to be most important?

To return to the end-of-unit test view of teaching and learning, the origin for this lies in a view of education which treats students as 'empty vessels', and where the job of the teacher is to 'pour in' as much 'knowledge' as possible. The function of assessment is to calculate what has gone in, from the perspective of how 'full' of knowledge the student has become. This view of assessment places the onus on the student to learn – to absorb – and the teacher to teach – to 'pour out' knowledge. This view does not dispute the status of knowledge – only high-status knowledge will do – and places most value on 'knowing that', as 'knowing how' is both difficult to teach, and problematic to test through pencil-and-paper means. This view of knowledge held sway for many years in the UK, and is looked back upon as the model of practice held by schools during a period up to about the end of the 1950s.

This simple and unproblematic view of school-valued knowledge as being 'knowing that' had, however, already begun to break down earlier in the twentieth century with a split between academic knowledge, as taught in grammar schools, and vocational learning, as delivered in secondary modern and technical schools. This split between academic (or technical) knowledge, and practical (or vocational) knowledge continues to this day, and causes occasional column inches in newspapers about how learning to change a wheel on a car can gain the learner an equivalent qualification level to understanding nuclear fission. This evaluation of the stratification of knowledge is itself problematic, as in contemporary society we need people who can change a wheel, as well as those who understand nuclear fission. But by evaluating, we place a value on, and this can involve making a judgement as to which is worth – literally, in future earning terms – more. As Freire (1985, p188) observed, 'education is a political act'. And it is not only education which is political. The notion that assessment too has political ramifications was noted by Broadfoot:

> *Assessment procedures are the vehicle whereby the dominant rationality of the corporate capitalist societies typical of the contemporary Western world is translated into the structures and processes of schooling.*
>
> (Broadfoot, 1999, p64)

This may seem like a complex and potentially contentious viewpoint with which to begin a book on assessment for trainee teachers. However, it is an important one for you to begin to think about. You have become a teacher by going through a system of education whereby you have been measured against your peers, and they (or maybe you!) have been found wanting in some respects. You have qualified (via assessments) to go into teaching, and have met, and will continue to have to meet, externally imposed standards (in your case, QTS) which legislate what you should know and have done, and what qualifications you should possess. There is a logic to this; after all a nation does not want its future left in hands of potentially unsound practitioners, just as it does not want its surgeons to be rank amateurs. So assessment, in this view, is used as a means to safeguard society.

PRACTICAL TASK PRACTICAL TASK PRACTICAL TASK PRACTICAL TASK PRACTICAL TASK

Your understandings of assessment
Here are some statements about assessment. As you read each, think about whether it rings true for you. In addition, try to think of some additional statements which are true for you to be added into each of the eight broad headings (labelled A–G).

A) Why do we assess?
1. To sort students out for future employment.
2. To assess how good a person they are.
3. To put them into teaching groups.
4. So that we know how well we have taught.
5. So that weak teachers can be 'weeded out'.
6. So we can change our units of work for what the students should do next.
7. So we have something to write on a report.
8. To find out what they know.
9. Because some students have to fail, so some can succeed.
10. To help students to learn.

B) What is assessment?
1. Giving tests.
2. Marking work.
3. Giving the right grade for a piece of work.
4. Talking to students about their work.
5. Using marking criteria properly.
6. Putting students into rank order.
7. Preparing students for the world of work.
8. Students talking to each other.
9. Maintaining social order.
10. Meeting national standards.

C) What is your role?
1. Giving your judgement about a student.
2. Acting as 'judge and jury'.
3. Giving the benefit of your experience and knowledge.
4. Telling the students how well or badly they have done in a test.
5. Collecting marks in your mark book.
6. Acting as an agent of the state in maintaining social order.
7. Marking tests.
8. Rewriting units of work in the light of students' comments.
9. Trying to guess what questions will be on the exam paper.
10. Knowing in what order things should be learned.

D) What is the role of the student – individually – collectively?

1. Answering test questions without cheating.

2. Accepting your judgement with regard to grades.

3. Knowing what they have to do to improve.

4. Telling you what they don't know or can't do.

5. Revising well.

6. Having good language skills in order to answer questions.

7. Allowing their more needy peers to have more of your time.

8. To learn what you teach.

9. Knowing how to learn.

10. Being able to apply learning in new situations.

E) What results from assessment?

1. Marks for your mark book.

2. GCSE/A level grades.

3. Better learning.

4. Knowing which the better schools are in an area.

5. Modifying your teaching to suit the needs of individuals.

6. Students having a better knowledge of what to do next.

7. Feelings of failure and/or resentment.

8. Students being able to proceed to the next stage of their learning.

9. The students knowing their place.

10. Knowing your classes better.

F) What will you do after assessment?

1. Make notes on your discussions with students.

2. Work out what to teach next.

3. Congratulate some students, commiserate with others.

4. Change your teaching strategy.

5. Enter the marks on a spreadsheet for possible use later.

6. Move on to the next topic.

7. Reflect on how well you taught that unit.

8. Compare results with colleagues.

9. Mark students' work.

10. Set targets.

G) What will the student(s) do after assessment?

1. Congratulate or commiserate with each other.

2. Reflect on what they have done.

3. Think about your comments.

4. Plan their future learning.

5. Look at the grade and ignore any comments.

6. Discuss their work with each other, reflecting on how to improve.

7. Think about how they learn.

8. Use their new knowledge/skills to good effect in their future work.

9. Try to contextualise their learning.

10. Do nothing.

Some of these statements have been deliberately provocative. This should prompt you into reflecting on a number of aspects of assessment. As you work your way through this book some of your assumptions might be challenged, your ideas on assessment changed, and your understandings of assessment developed.

We will revisit aspects of this practical task in the final chapter, when we think about your future development.

Uses and purposes of assessment

Our next consideration is that of the uses and purposes of assessment. TGAT, the Task Group on Assessment and Testing report (TGAT, 1988) described four purposes for assessment. These are:

- **formative;**
- **summative;**
- **diagnostic;**
- **evaluative.**

Formative and summative assessment we shall discuss in Chapters 4 and 3 respectively, although it is interesting to note that it was the TGAT report that propelled these terminologies into widespread educational parlance. The purpose of diagnostic assessment was to diagnose learning difficulties in the individual student, so that appropriate interventions could be planned and executed. Nowadays diagnostic assessment is generally subsumed within formative assessment. Evaluative assessment is that which evaluates the success of a whole school. More recently it has also been used as the means by which teachers evaluate the success of learning programmes. The TGAT report has been influential in terms of assessment research and particularly for describing and labelling different purposes for assessment. The full recommendations of the TGAT report, some might argue, have not been followed up, but its influence on nomenclature and thinking has been significant.

Other commentators on purposes of assessment include Lambert and Lines (2000), who also suggest four purposes for assessment, three of which are very much in line with the TGAT, but Lambert and Lines replace 'diagnostic', which they include under formative, with 'certification', which they define as 'the means for selecting by qualification' (Lambert and Lines, 2000, p4). This aspect of assessment will be discussed further in Chapter 3, which focuses on summative assessment.

Uses of assessment

These distinctions between purposes of assessment are useful for teachers, but it is the use to which teachers put the information gained from them that is likely to be the most important aspect for your work in the classroom. After all:

These terms are therefore not descriptions of kinds of assessment, but rather of the use to which information arising from the assessments is put.

(Weeden et al., 2002, p19)

The uses which you as a beginning teacher are able to make of assessment information are matters which we shall be considering throughout this book. However, it is clear, even at this early stage, that what we can say is that uses of assessment information are manifold.

REFLECTIVE TASK

Think of three uses of assessment information which you have seen, or used yourself.

There are many possible responses to this reflective task. However, what is most apposite to consider is the use to which your assessment information is put. Day-to-day assessment should help teachers and students in a day-to-day fashion. 'Big' outcomes are only needed occasionally. Assessment should provide information which means something to the participants. There is an old saying to the effect that 'weighing the pig doesn't make it any fatter'. This is true in education too: a teacher may test their students' knowledge every day, but what is likely to really make a difference is if the students learn something in between the tests. It could be argued in this instance that greater gains could be made if the teacher were to teach more and test less. We can also wonder about what happens to all the marks gained in these tests. If they are simply entered into a mark book, then no real use is being made of the assessment data. For example, consider the following:

Got full marks on the Geography test today. Yes! I am proud to report that I got twenty out of twenty!... There is nothing I don't know about the Norwegian leather industry.

(Townsend, 1982)

Adrian Mole's observation that there is 'nothing he does not know' here is obviously flawed. But what is the result from his test telling him, and what is it telling his teacher? Here, again, we want to know what use is made of the assessment data.

REFLECTIVE TASK

Look back at the last reflective task. What use was made of the assessment information you described? If it vanished into a mark book, ask yourself why?

Let us return to Adrian Mole's test, and try to unpick some further details. We, as outsiders, need to know a lot more about it. For example, what sort of test was it, what sort of questions were asked, was it multiple-choice or long answer, and would he get the same scores again? These questions take us into the areas of reliability and validity. These are both key notions with regards to assessment, so we shall consider them each in turn.

Reliability

Reliability refers to consistency of assessment results. Examples include the following.

- **If the same person undertook an assessment on subsequent days, would he or she get the same results?**

- If different people marked the assessment would the results be the same? (This is known as *inter-rater reliability*.)
- If the same person marked an assessment on different occasions, would the same results be reached? (*intra-rater reliability.)*
- If an assessment was undertaken by a similar group of students, would they achieve the same results? *(inter-cohort reliability.)*

The implications of this are that reliability:

> *... is concerned with precision and accuracy. Some features, e.g. height, can be measured accurately, whilst others, e.g. musical ability, cannot.*
>
> (Cohen *et al.*, 2000, p117)

Validity

Validity refers to whether or not an assessment measures what it sets out to measure. McCormick and James (1983), and James (1998) discuss a number of categories of validity in terms of how they relate to assessments. From your perspective as a beginning teacher four main areas of validity can be said to be applicable to the ways in which you think about the assessment materials that you will use with your students.

1. Face validity: This is where an assessment looks as if it is assessing that which it is supposed to be assessing.
2. Content validity: Here the data need to be relevant to the subject matter. However, an easy option here is to assess 'knowing that', rather than 'knowing how to'.
3. Predictive validity. This is where the validity of an assessment is determined by its ability to predict future attainment.
4. Construct validity: This relates to content validity in many ways, and some view it as a wider frame of reference. So, for example, in history an assessment should be assessing notions of historical import, rather than, say, the ability to read the question.

From these categories of validity it is possible to investigate assessment procedures to see whether, and to what extent, they are met. These may seem like issues which are distant from your everyday practice in schools, but this is not necessarily the case.

REFLECTIVE TASK

Take as an example an assessment you have made of a student's learning. Did you base your assessment on a true judgement of their knowledge in the domain in question, or was your assessment based upon their ability to accurately describe things in good English?

If, in fact, the assessment was based on language skills, then it can be said to have poor face, content and construct validity. Let us take the case of a PE teacher instructing her students in throwing the javelin. Upon what will her assessments be based? Hopefully, it will be based upon her observations of her students and, when they are good enough, of them taking part in competitive throwing events. She is unlikely to assess them by asking them to write an essay entitled 'How to throw the javelin'. This may seem an extreme example, but you need to give very careful thought to your own assessments to make sure you are not falling into the trap of assessing language instead of subject knowledge.

From this discussion, it should be apparent that reliability and validity are linked in that both should be present in order for an assessment to be deemed worthwhile. However, there can be trade-offs, in that we want our assessments to be worthwhile, but achievable:

> *... quality in assessment is the provision of information of the highest validity and optimum reliability suited to a particular purpose and context.*
>
> (Harlen 1994, p13)

As a way of illustrating this, let us take an exemplar case study away from education, and consider the UK driving test. This is an assessment of an individual's capability and competence at driving a car. It is also summative, in that it can normally be expected to take place at the end of a formal period of instruction. The driving test appears to be valid on a number of counts: it assesses driving by asking the candidate to drive, it assesses knowing that road signs have specific meanings, and knowing how in terms of the process of driving. However, is it reliable? If a candidate took a test and failed today, might they pass tomorrow? Anecdotally there are many stories to this effect. Can the location where you take it make a difference? One year the pass rate in Lerwick in the Shetland Islands was 72.3 per cent; in Brentwood in Essex the pass rate was 27.1 per cent. Are Essex drivers not as good or well prepared as Shetland Islanders, or are other factors coming into play here? One might ask, for example, whether driving conditions in Lerwick are comparable with those near London.

REFLECTIVE TASK

If the pass rates for Lerwick and Brentwood driving test centres were school league table results, would they mean something different?

So, from the example of the driving test, we can see that it is possible to have a valid assessment which is not necessarily highly reliable. In your work there will be similar issues, for example Class 9X and Class 9Z will contain different individuals, and your lessons, although covering the same topic, will also have been different, due to the natural ebb and flow of teaching and learning with different cohorts. Conducting the same assessments with both classes may well produce different results. Multiply this by classes being taught by different teachers, and in different schools, and you will begin to appreciate some of the potential problems. However, it is important to note that you will be most concerned with things going on in your school, and in your classroom, and that for normal everyday purposes your concerns will be with materials you use and, as we discussed above, the uses you make of the assessment data you get. As Harlen noted in the extract cited earlier this will be your context, and it is this which will matter to you. It also means that reliability is increased, as the assessments which you use will have a common factor – you.

Your use of assessment

From these discussions it should be clear that assessment is complex, and that there are many issues you will need to think about in order to use assessment effectively. We shall move in subsequent chapters towards a consideration of formative and summative purposes of assessment for you in your context. Before we do that, however, we need to return to our philosophical discussion from the opening of this chapter. At the stage of being a beginning teacher, broad considerations of assessment issue will doubtless take a back seat in comparison with your concerns about day-to-day classroom matters, issues connected with behaviour management, and what you can do about the learning of individual students in your class. This is what your mentors and those working with you will expect. What this does mean, picking up the final point from the last paragraph, is that as your concerns should be with what works for you, then you ought to be able to construct assessments which are reliable and valid in your context, in that you are the stable linking factor.

Contextualising assessment within teaching and learning

One of the approaches which we will be advocating throughout this book is the notion of linking assessment very closely with teaching and learning. Figure 1.1 showed how traditionally assessment and instruction were separate activities. We are suggesting that in many cases, particularly with regard to the effective use of formative assessment, that you consider planning for assessment alongside your planning for teaching and learning. This means that the model of assessment, and teaching and learning, will now look more like that which is represented in Figure 1.3.

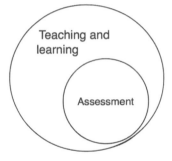

Figure 1.3 Assessment within teaching and learning

This shows that assessment is integral to teaching and learning. This way of viewing assessment provides other benefits too, in that using assessment data and feeding it back into your teaching becomes a routine part of your work. This has the added effect of helping you target specific teaching to where it is most needed:

> *Instructional assessment provides an opportunity for teachers to explore the nature, structure, and products of their teaching. It becomes a reflective activity that informs instruction...*

> (Graue, 1993, p285)

Reflection is a key feature in your development as a beginning teacher, and any opportunity that presents itself for you to reflect on teaching and learning is to be welcomed. This will evidence itself in the lesson evaluations that you will normally be required to submit, and in documentation you keep for in-school assessment purposes.

Conclusion

This chapter has presented a lot of information, and introduced some complex discussions. This has been necessary to equip you to continue with your voyage into the issues surrounding assessment in education today. In subsequent chapters we turn to a more direct consideration of issues with specific purposes and uses of assessment, and how these will be of benefit to you in the classroom.

A SUMMARY OF **KEY POINTS**

We have considered how views of teaching, learning and assessment are all inextricably bound up one with another. We have discussed a philosophy of assessment where useful and usable results are achieved. We are now in a position to note that this emerging philosophy involves assessment:

> **being integrated with teaching and learning;**

> **activities being as reliable and valid as possible;**

> **having relevance to your own context;**

> **being purposeful – providing data which has meaning to teacher (you) and students;**

> **providing a basis on which future teaching and learning can be built.**

We have noted that assessment purposes include:
> **summative assessment;**

> **formative assessment.**

And we have noted that assessment uses are the ways in which you will derive information from assessments – formal, informal, summative and formative – and employ these with the students you teach.

REFERENCES REFERENCES **REFERENCES** REFERENCES **REFERENCES** REFERENCES

Broadfoot, P. (1999) Assessment and the emergence of modern society, in Moon, B. and Murphy, P. (eds) *Curriculum in context*. London: Paul Chapman/Open University.

Cohen, L., Manion, L. and Morrison, R. (2000) *Research methods in education* (5th edition). London: RoutledgeFalmer.

Freire, P. (1985) *The politics of education: culture, power, and liberation*. Hadley, Mass.: Bergin & Garvey.

Graue, M. (1993) Integrating theory and practice through instructional assessment. *Educational Assessment*, **1**: 283–309.

Harlen, W. (1994) *Enhancing quality in assessment*. London: Paul Chapman.

James, M. (1998) *Using assessment for school improvement*. Oxford: Heinemann Educational.

Lambert, D. and Lines, D. (2000) *Understanding assessment: purposes, perceptions, practice*. London: RoutledgeFalmer.

McCormick, R. and James, M. (1983) *Curriculum evaluation in schools*. Beckenham: Croom Helm.

Ryle, G. (1949) *The concept of mind*. London: Penguin Books.

TGAT (1988) *Task Group on Assessment and Testing: A report*. London: DES.

Townsend, S. (1982) *The secret diary of Adrian Mole aged 13³/₄*. London: Methuen.

Weeden, P., Winter, J. and Broadfoot, P. (2002) *Assessment – What's in it for schools?*. London, New York: RoutledgeFalmer.

Young, M. (ed) (1971) *Knowledge and control*. London: Collier-Macmillan.

Young, M. (1999) The curriculum as socially organised knowledge, in McCormick, R. and Paechter, C. (eds) *Learning and Knowledge*. London: Paul Chapman/Open University.

FURTHER READING FURTHER READING **FURTHER READING** FURTHER READING

Black, P. (1999) Assessment, Learning theories and testing systems, in Murphy, P. (ed) *Learners, learning and assessment*, pp18–34. London: Paul Chapman.

Weeden, P., Winter, J. and Broadfoot, P. (2002) *Assessment – What's in it for schools?* London, New York: RoutledgeFalmer.

2
Theoretical approaches to learning and assessment

Chapter objectives

By the end of this chapter you should have:

- **learned about different theoretical approaches to learning;**
- **considered how different views of learning affect assessment;**
- **considered the nature of knowledge.**

Professional Standards for QTS

This chapter will help you to meet the following Professional Standards for QTS:
Q7a, Q10, Q12, Q26a-b

Introduction

We saw in the opening chapter how learning, knowledge, and assessment are interlinked. In order to understand fully what it is that you are doing when you teach and assess, it is appropriate to consider theoretical approaches to learning and knowledge, and it is to that which we now turn. We know already that assessment is concerned with making judgements, and thinking about theoretical matters will help you contextualise the assessments you make on a daily basis in the classroom. It will also enable you to realise how differing views of learning and knowledge tend to lead towards different types of assessments. This is not an isolated academic discussion, but has real bearing on the ways in which assessments are constructed, and the ways in which certain types of knowledge are valued and tested for. This has real implications for your work in the classroom.

Learning theory

Learning theory endeavours to describe the ways in which people learn things. This is pertinent to our discussions because, as we shall see, different theoretical stances give rise to different views of knowledge, and to different types of assessment with which to evaluate acquisition of this knowledge. There are many different individual learning theories accounting for different aspects of learning. For the sake of simplicity we are going to group theories into five main types. These are:

- **behaviourism;**
- **cognitive developmentalism and constructivism;**
- **social constructivism;**
- **multiple intelligences;**
- **information processing and brain-based approaches.**

We shall examine each of these in turn, and discuss views of assessment that each different family of theories might be considered as giving rise to. Before we do this, however, it is worth noting that:

> ... *learning theorists themselves rarely make statements about how learning outcomes within their models should be assessed.*
>
> (James, 2006, p47)

Therefore, we will, to some extent, be engaging in a *post hoc*, or 'after the event', discussion concerning assessment, and of how different assessment opportunities can be seen to arise from the learning theories which we describe.

Behaviourism

The essential feature of behaviourist views of learning is that learning should be considered in terms of evidence of behaviours. This is fairly obvious when considering things like throwing a javelin, where a specific set of bodily-muscular movements are required to effect the throw; but it is less obvious when thinking about what is going on when learners are doing something like, say, long division. Strict behaviourists would say that the individual concerned has acquired the habits necessary to do long division, as they insist that the mind (the term used by behaviourists is 'mentalism') is not involved to any great extent. This divorcing of the brain from behaviour is a key feature of this way of considering learning.

Much of the early work on behaviourism was done with animals. Pavlov's dogs salivating due to the stimulus of a bell being rung while they were fed is a famous example. This Pavlovian response relies on *conditioning*, where wanted behaviours are *reinforced*, and unwanted behaviours receive *negative reinforcement* or punishment. These principles were applied to human learning too. Although behaviourism has had a bit of a 'bad press' in some educational quarters during recent years, aspects of behaviourist approaches can be seen in schools on a daily basis; and wanted behaviours, such as not shouting at the teacher, staying in a seat when required, and not running in corridors are reinforced, often, it has to be said, by applying negative reinforcement (punishment) to unwanted behaviours, but also, for example by the use of praise, when desired behaviours warrant positive attention. Indeed, the use of positive reinforcement for wanted behaviours figures highly in many contemporary training programmes for behaviour management.

What behaviourism is not

A common misconception often encountered among trainee teachers is that behaviourism is about getting students to behave well. This is not the case, however desirable an outcome this may be. Behaviourism is concerned with behaviours in the sense of human or animal actions which can be observed. Such actions are said to be behaviours. So playing cricket involves a set of behaviours, as does flying a kite, playing the piano, or riding a bike.

Breaking down learning

The behaviourist approach to learning takes the view that complex tasks are best broken down into smaller sub-routines, which need to be mastered sequentially. This approach is applied to both skills, which can be thought of as observed behaviours when they are practical, and knowledge, which in a behaviourist view often involves the memorising of sequences of facts. For the teacher, the role adopted is that of instructor. The instructor breaks down a skill into small sections and teaches these individually and sequentially. Thus

17

in learning to drive, the mastery of clutch movement and gear changing is a skill which needs to be practised before full control of the car can be said to take place. This is one of many behaviours which needs mastering before a student can be entered for a driving test.

You have probably noted that driving involves a number of behaviours. Aside from clutch control and gear changing, which we have already mentioned, there are also steering, using the handbrake, using the accelerator, looking in the mirror, and many, many more.

Assessment implications of behaviourism

Assessment viewed from a behaviourist perspective involves making judgements about observable behaviours, and ascertaining whether or not the student can evidence the required behaviour. Reinforcing desired behaviours, and trying to eradicate unwanted ones, result from the teacher (acting in accordance with school policies in many cases) making a judgement, and delivering the results to the individual concerned. In the example of the javelin mentioned in Chapter 1, the PE teacher concerned will be assessing the javelin-throwing behaviours of her students. She will be thinking about how they threw the javelin, what they need to do to get better at throwing it, and will try to make them aware that in this sport it is the distance thrown that matters, and that this is achieved through a balance of technique and skill. The assessments she makes will be of practical actions, and these will be intended to help the students get better at throwing. These will include formative assessments, another key assessment term. These formative assessments help the student and the teacher know what to do next to improve. It would be pointless if the PE teacher only ever measured the distance the javelin went (i.e. only made summative assessments). She wants to help the students get better, and to do this she needs to intervene appropriately in the process. Formative assessment is bound up with a way of viewing teaching and learning, and will figure prominently in Chapter 4, and elsewhere throughout this book. Put simply, for the moment, summative assessment looks back on achievements made, and formative assessment looks forward to developing future achievement.

From a classical behaviourist stance, educational assessment techniques are often built around such things as short-answer questions, multiple choice and true/false tests. These are often timed, rather than open-ended, sometimes with different timings for different sections. The answers required are generally closed, with a right/wrong marking scheme.

In this view it is the individual student who acquires, or fails to acquire in some instances, the necessary skills. These are tested for in the ways described above. If the individual passes the test, all is well, and they can proceed to the next stage of sequenced learning. What happens in the case of those who do not meet requirements is that as they have not achieved, they will need to be re-instructed, and then retested. Otherwise, they are likely to have an insecure knowledge base for future learning. In some school systems this might mean having to retake a programme, sometimes a whole school year. This outcome is very rare in the UK, but far more common elsewhere, particularly in such countries as the United States of America.

Cognitive developmentalism and constructivism

In some senses, the Swiss educationalist Piaget developed a theoretical approach to learning which stands in opposition to behaviourism, in that he described how students' cognitive abilities develop as they mature (Piaget, 1952 *inter alia*). This is known as his *stage theory of development*. In this view of learning, the brain is involved, and, as well as this, interactions with others are seen to be important. The mental activities which the child uses, known as *operations*, change with age; young children, for example, being unable to recognise that others can have a viewpoint which is different from their own. Originally Piaget placed specific age ranges on the stages he proposed, an aspect of his work which was criticised for being too rigid. This aspect of his work was later revised, and nowadays Neo-Piagetian approaches follow the broad outline of stages of development, but remove the age-specificity by saying that stages occur, but at different times in different individuals.

One of the important outcomes of Piaget's work is that growing up from a young child to a teenager does not just mean that the individual knows more, but that there are changes in the way in which thinking itself takes place. Constructivist views of learning centre on the notion that learning is an active process, and one in which the individual constructs meaning for themselves:

> *Students actively construct... ways of knowing as they strive to be effective by restoring coherence to the worlds of their personal experience.*
>
> (Cobb, 1999, p135)

This means that the mind plays an important role in the process of learning, by constructing meaning for itself. This might seem an obvious way of looking at things, but contrast it with the behaviourist perspective where tasks are broken down, lists of facts learnt, and the mind is not considered as important as observable behaviours.

Assessment implications of cognitive developmentalism and constructivism

From an assessment perspective, one of the things which we can take from Piaget's work is the notion of cognitive readiness, and of ensuring that the work presented to the students presents sufficient by way of cognitive challenge, as well as being appropriate for the students in terms of their cognitive development. There is a role here for assessments in which the teacher makes judgements concerning the readiness of the students for the work they need to do.

Social constructivism

Social constructivism takes as its basic tenet the notion that learning takes place as learners actively construct meanings from their dealings with others. The work of Vygotsky, who was active as a psychologist in the Soviet Union in the 1930s (although his work did not become known in the West until much later), is central to this way of looking at learning. For Vygotsky, speech was central to development and he believed that speech (both out loud, and silent, internal speech) facilitated thinking. One of Vygotsky's main contributions to the literature on learning is his well-known notion of the *zone of proximal development* (ZPD). This is defined as being:

> ...the distance between the actual developmental level as determined by independent problem solving and the level of potential development as determined through problem solving under adult guidance, or in collaboration with more capable peers.

> (Vygotsky, 1978, p86)

What this means is that a child is able to achieve at a higher level when working alongside someone who is more experienced than they are, either an adult or another student. This view of learning and knowledge can be seen to encompass both 'knowing that' and 'knowing how', and, in common with the views of Piaget above, will inevitably involve speech as a communicative tool. This is an aspect which we explore later. The notion of the ZPD means that group work is an important factor in learning, as students are able to evidence achievement at a higher level when working co-operatively.

REFLECTIVE TASK

Think back on an example of when you observed students working together on a task in groups. Are you able to think of examples of ZPD learning which shows that a student was working at a higher level in this fashion?

Vygotsky also said (with the gender specificity not uncommon of his time) that the ZPD was a useful stage in the development of autonomous achievement:

> What the child is able to do in collaboration today he will be able to do independently tomorrow.

> (Vygotsky, 1987, p211)

Discussions of students learning through experience, and working with others, also appear in the work of the American psychologist Jerome Bruner. Bruner postulated that developing cognitive structures within the child enable complex ideas to be revisited at different stages of individuals' academic studies. He proposed that the scholastic organisation of this should be in the form of a *spiral curriculum*, where there is movement both horizontally and vertically. This means that topics should be covered more than once, in different depths according to the cognitive readiness of the students:

> A curriculum as it develops should revisit the basic ideas repeatedly, building upon them until the student has grasped the full formal apparatus that goes with them.

> (Bruner, 1960, p13)

A simple graphical representation of a spiral curriculum is shown in Figure 2.1.

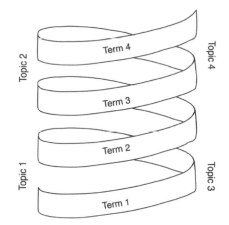

Figure 2.1 The spiral curriculum

Assessment implications of social constructivist approaches

There are many opportunities for assessment within this view of education. The role of groupwork as an aid to learning can present particular challenges for summative assessment of individuals, but has a great deal to offer in terms of potential for formative assessment.

PRACTICAL TASK PRACTICAL TASK **PRACTICAL TASK** PRACTICAL TASK **PRACTICAL TASK**

Devise and carry out a group learning opportunity which your students can undertake in one of your forthcoming units of work. As the students do it, listen to the discussions that are taking place. If you say anything to them, think about what you are saying – what is the purpose of your interjection?

However, it is not only in groupwork that social constructivist notions operate, as learning is conceived as a social activity, with the individual acting as a member of a group. This contrasts with the individual meaning made under constructivism.

Multiple intelligences

Howard Gardner's work with multiple intelligences is concerned with how individuals have differing abilities in differing domains. Traditional IQ tests tended to measure mathematical/ linguistic aptitudes, and provide a single IQ score for this. Gardner said that achievement was not confined solely to these areas, and that people displayed a variety of 'intelligences' in differing degrees. He stated that there are nine potential intelligences that can be observed (Gardner, 1983, 1999).

- *Verbal-linguistic intelligence – well-developed verbal skills and sensitivity to the sounds, meanings and rhythms of words.*
- *Mathematical-logical intelligence – ability to think conceptually and abstractly, and able to discern logical or numerical patterns.*
- *Musical intelligence – ability to produce and appreciate rhythm, pitch and timbre.*
- *Visual-spatial intelligence – capacity to think in images and pictures, to visualise accurately and abstractly.*
- *Bodily-kinesthetic intelligence – ability to control one's body movements and to handle objects skilfully.*

- *Interpersonal intelligence – capacity to detect and respond appropriately to the moods, motivations and feelings of others.*
- *Intrapersonal Intelligence – capacity to be self-aware and in tune with own inner feelings, values, beliefs and thinking processes.*
- *Naturalist intelligence – ability to recognise and categorise plants, animals and other objects in nature.*
- *Existential intelligence – sensitivity and capacity to tackle deep questions about human existence, such as the meaning of life, why do we die, and how did we get here.*

(Fautley and Savage, 2007, p44)

This forms the basis of Gardner's multiple intelligence (MI) theory. In assessment terms, teachers may make judgements about where an individual student's intelligences may lie, but within this the whole range of assessment opportunities is available. It may be that in groupwork activities specific attributes are deemed worthwhile, but teachers need to be aware that Gardner himself has been scathing of programmes of study being built on his work. As he put it:

I learned that an entire state had adapted an education programme based in part on MI theory ... The more I learned about this programme, the less comfortable I was. Much of it was a mishmash of practices – left brain and right brain contrasts, sensory learning styles, neurolinguistic programming and multiple intelligences approaches, all mixed with dazzling promiscuity.

(Revell, 2005)

Assessment implications of MI approaches

Tests are available for multiple intelligences, but these lie beyond normal classroom assessment practice in terms of formative or summative purposes. Some educational programmes have included the notion of MI alongside learning styles, or learning preferences, including VAK (visual–auditory–kinaesthetic) learning. Again, assessments can be devised for these, but from your perspective as a beginning teacher what will be of most benefit is likely to be using information gained about students in as many ways as possible. This is another topic to which we shall return in Chapter 6.

Information processing and brain-based approaches

Early work on artificial intelligence investigated ways in which learning could be broken down so as to become a series of 'rules' with which a computer can be programmed to 'learn' how to perform tasks. This is known as the information processing (IP) model of learning; it is also referred to by (Bruner, 1999, p148) as a *computational view of mind*. In this view of learning there are three main stages.

- **Encoding: Where information taken in is processed for storage. This stage is undertaken by the *sensory register* (sometimes referred to as *sensory buffer*).**
- **Storage: here information is 'filed' for storage in either the *long-term* or *short-term* memory.**
- **Retrieval: Information learned is brought out of storage.**

The IP model is represented diagrammatically in Figure 2.2.

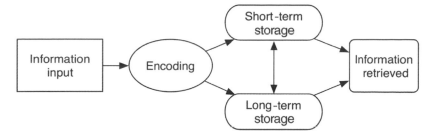

Figure 2.2 Information processing

With the developing knowledge of how the brain works that contemporary neuroscience is revealing, recent approaches to learning have considered how this information can be used to make learning ever more effective. One UK approach which is to some extent brain-based is the *building learning power* (BLP) work of Guy Claxton and his team from Bristol University (Claxton, 2002). Many schools are becoming involved, and yours may be one. This adopts an approach based on developing the power of learners to maximise their own learning potential.

Our knowledge of cognitive neuroscience is a still-developing area. In the domain of education a number of secondary programmes, not sanctioned by the original researchers, have been built on what the Teaching and Learning Research Programme refers to as 'neuro-myths' (TLRP, 2007). From your perspective, as a beginning teacher, you should be aware that there is, as yet, no 'magic bullet' which offers direct access to the human brain for learning.

Assessment implications of IP and brain-based approaches

Summative assessment viewed from this approach is concerned with finding out what students know; formative assessment is concerned with helping with encoding and storage of information, for subsequent retrieval. What we can take from brain-based approaches is that the notions of information storage and retrieval are important ones. This in turn helps explain why we need to consider teaching and learning as separate, but linked, processes. An important mantra for this book is the notion that:

$$Teaching \neq Learning$$
('Teaching does not equal learning')

In brain-based approaches we can see that, however secure our view of sequential learning is, the best planned and executed teaching programme ever devised does not mean that there will be a shortcut to the minds of the students.

Synthesising views of learning

Looking back over these views of learning, it may seem confusing that a number of different theoretical approaches are trying, in their various ways, to explain the same thing. It is also important to note that teachers take and use parts of many theories in their day to day work in the classroom, in other words, that:

> . . . no one theory has provided all the answers to the kinds of questions of concern to teachers.

(Child, 1997, p113)

REFLECTIVE TASK

(Metacognitive activity)
We began by discussing the philosophical location of assessment. As we have discussed different views of learning, think about how your own views on assessment have developed.

Discussion

Theoretical considerations may seem a long way removed from your daily existence, particularly when you are grappling with a Year 9 class on a wet Friday afternoon! However, they are important in that they inform ways in which teaching, learning and assessment operate. As a teacher you are dealing with 'knowledge', and as we discuss in a number of chapters in this book and elsewhere, knowledge is itself a problematic construct. This means that you really need to understand 'the knowledge' that you are imparting, and that the students are learning. For some of the views of learning we have looked at in this section, there can at times be very little by way of connection between what you want to teach, and what the students have learned:

> *Within education, constructivist ideas are translated as meaning that all learners actually construct knowledge for themselves, rather than knowledge coming from the teacher and being 'absorbed' by the student. This means that every student will learn something slightly different from a given lesson, and that as a teacher we can never be certain what our students will learn.*
>
> (Muijs and Reynolds, 2005, p62)

Later on in Chapter 5, we will look at learning outcomes. Here, it is useful to note that what happens in these can be tangential to our intentions as teachers. What is important is to disentangle the methodical nature of planning for teaching, and the less linear journey the learner takes.

CLASSROOM STORY

One of the authors of this book recently went to a lecture on learning. Here is his story:

> *I went to listen to a lecture on learning which was being given to a group of teachers and academics. Being interested in the subject I thought I would try to operate at a meta-level, and endeavour to think about my learning about learning. What happened was this: I quickly learned that the flip-up seats in the lecture theatre were very uncomfortable. The next thing I learned was that when the kitchen delivery lorry was unloading, I couldn't hear a thing. I also learned that having too much text on a Powerpoint slide meant I couldn't read it properly when sitting at the back. Next I learned that the graffiti on the lecture theatre desks was quite intriguing, and that one of the students playing Frisbee on the grass outside was useless at it! None of these had anything to do with the lecture, but I learned them anyway!*

This could well be the case for the students in your classroom too. There are many factors you need to take into account when planning for learning, but even so there will be times when you can have little control over the realities of what is learned.

PRACTICAL TASK PRACTICAL TASK **PRACTICAL TASK** PRACTICAL TASK **PRACTICAL TASK**

During a plenary session in one of your lessons, try asking a class of students to reflect on their own learning. Encourage them to be creative in the manner of the story above, and find out what they can identify that they have learned. You might be surprised at the results.

Conclusion

We have seen how different views of learning give rise to different ways of assessing knowledge. Theoretical views account for things, and having an understanding of them can help you to understand your own practice. However, at this stage in your development you are likely to be most concerned with day-to-day issues of 'what works', and so will be eclectic in your approach, taking a little from each of the theoretical approaches as appropriate to the task in hand. For example, if you are involved in teaching skills you will take bits of behaviourism; if you are teaching difficult concepts you may want the students to talk about these to each other, and so will use socially constructed aspects of learning. This syncretic approach is fine, and is appropriate to the complex reality of life in the contemporary classroom.

A SUMMARY OF **KEY POINTS**

In this chapter you have:
> **learned about different families of learning theories;**
> **thought about the ways in which views of learning and knowledge affect the ways assessment takes place;**
> **considered that learning might not be a linear process;**
> **probably learned a lot things we had not foreseen too.**

REFERENCES REFERENCES **REFERENCES** REFERENCES **REFERENCES** REFERENCES

Bruner, J. (1999) Culture, mind, and education, in Moon, B. and Murphy, P. (eds) *Curriculum in context*. London: Paul Chapman/Open University.

Bruner, J.S. (1960) *The process of education*. Cambridge, Mass.: Harvard University Press.

Child, D. (1997) *Psychology and the teacher* (6th edition). London: Cassell.

Claxton, G. (2002) *Building learning power: helping young people become better learners*. Bristol: TLO.

Cobb, P. (1999) Where is the Mind?, in Murphy, P. (ed) *Learners, learning and assessment,* pp 135–50. London: Paul Chapman/Open University.

Fautley, M. and Savage, J. (2007) *Creativity in secondary education*. Exeter: Learning Matters.

Gardner, H. (1983) *Frames of mind*. London: Heinemann.

Gardner, H. (1999) *Intelligence reframed*. New York: Basic Books.

James, M. (2006) Assessment, teaching and theories of learning, in Gardner, J. (ed) *Assessment and learning.* London: SAGE.

Muijs, D. and Reynolds, D. (2005) *Effective teaching: evidence and practice*. London: SAGE Publications.

Piaget, J. (1952) *The origin of intelligence in the child*. London: Routledge and Kegan Paul.

Revell, P. (2005) Each to their own. *Guardian,* London.

TLRP (2007) Neuroscience and education: issues and opportunities. **www.tlrp.org/pub/documents/ Neuroscience%20Commentary%20FINAL.pdf** accessed June 2007

Vygotsky, L. (1978) *Mind in society*. Cambridge, Mass.: Harvard University Press.

Vygotsky, L. (1987) *The collected works, Vol 1*. New York: Plenum.

FURTHER READING FURTHER READING **FURTHER READING** FURTHER READING

Black, P. (1999) Assessment, learning theories and testing systems, in Murphy, P. (ed) *Learners, learning and assessment*, pp 118–34. London: Paul Chapman/Open University.

Gardner, H. (1999) Assessment in context, in Murphy, P. (ed) *Learners, learning and assessment*. London: Paul Chapman/Open University.

3
Summative assessment

Introduction

We have already discussed in the opening part of this book how one of the main features of summative assessment is that it looks back on achievement. In a way, the judgements and marks which arrive from using summative assessment can be viewed as a summing-up of a student's achievement. This is an important point to reiterate. Summative assessment looks back on achievement, and this distinguishes it from formative assessment, which, as we shall see in the next chapter, is essentially about using assessment to look forward.

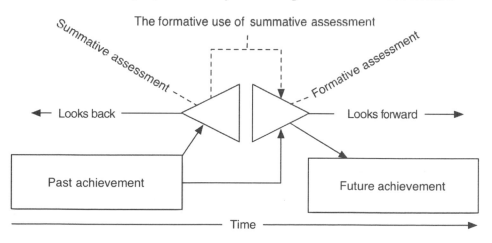

Figure 3.1 Assessment modalities

Figure 3.1 shows formative and summative assessments. It also shows using summative assessment for formative purposes, which is an increasingly important way of using summative assessment to inform teachers and students in what steps to take to develop future learning.

For many years, summative assessments were the mainstay of the teacher's repertoire of assessment techniques.

> ## REFLECTIVE TASK
>
> Think back to your own schooldays. Can you think of different types of summative assessments that you were given?

In response to this reflective task, maybe you thought about the high-stakes assessments, public examinations such as GCSE and A level. Perhaps you thought about tests, maybe end-of-term or end-of-unit. Some of you may have considered practical examinations which you had to take, perhaps involving cake making or car mechanics. Whatever it was that you considered, the essential feature of summative assessment is, as we have seen, that teaching occurs 'curiously separate' from assessment. So, how can summative assessment be of use to you in the classroom, what will you use it for, and what will happen to the results? These are important questions, but the answers to them are not necessarily simple and straightforward.

Marking and grading

Let us begin with one of the everyday summative assessments which you will come across in schools: marking and grading individual pieces of students' work.

> ## REFLECTIVE TASK
>
> Think about marking and grading the following original pieces of work.
> 1. A story in English.
> 2. A page of sums in mathematics.
> 3. A written description of a physics experiment.
> 4. The physics experiment itself.
> 5. A painting of a tree in art.
> 6. A description of going shopping in French.
> 7. A poem about rain.

Did you find yourself thinking about what the teacher would be looking for in each of these cases? Maybe you were wondering about what the teacher had in mind when setting the task. Perhaps you were thinking about tasks like this from your own schooldays. An important consideration in all of the seven examples above is that of the distinction between marking and grading. Marking a story in English is likely to involve the teacher making a series of different decisions from the maths teacher marking a page of sums. The English teacher is likely to comment on the quality of the ideas as well as on spelling and punctuation. The maths teacher will be looking for the way the student has arrived at the answer, as well as the correctness of answers themselves. Grading each of these pieces of work will involve different decisions too. So, if marking some of the pieces of work involves a decision concerning quality, what is the teacher doing to arrive at this? The usual way that this takes place is via a form of criterion referencing. The teacher has a list, or makes judgements against their impressions, of what should be contained in an answer. This list of criteria will inform the grade which results.

Suppose that each piece of work received the grade of seven out of ten. What would that tell the teacher and student? Supposing instead each piece of work received the grade B+. Is this the same?

Your answer to this will depend on what you believe the criteria to have been. A common assumption, often untrue, is that grades in mathematics reflect the number of correct answers a student has achieved. If this was the criterion that you used for item 2 in the list above, then you will have assumed that the student answered seven sums correctly out of a total of ten. For item 7, the poem, you are likely to have decided that the criteria related to correctness of form, and quality of ideas. The issue of quality is problematic in some areas of work. Item 5, the painting, may have presented non-art teachers with a problem. What happens, you might think, if you do not like the work which the student has done? For art teachers, the notion of *connoisseurship* means that the teacher is hopefully able to transcend value judgements, and arrive at a more reasoned response.

REFLECTIVE TASK

Think about quality in your own subject area.
What is quality?
How do you know?
How can you share this with the students?
How can you reflect this in your grading system?

This may not be as straightforward as you first thought. It is also a philosophical question that has exercised many minds over the centuries.

The issue of quality

Quality – you know what it is, yet you don't know what it is. But that's self-contradictory. But some things are better than others, that is, they have more quality. But when you try to say what the quality is, apart from the things that have it, it all goes poof! There's nothing to talk about. But if you can't say what Quality is, how do you know what it is, or how do you know that it even exists? If no one knows what it is, then for all practical purposes it doesn't exist at all. But for all practical purposes it really does exist. What else are the grades based on?

(Pirsig, 1974, p187)

As Pirsig says, 'what else are the grades based on?' You will need to decide what criteria for quality you will use in your marking and grading. This is likely to be subject dependent, and has the potential for being a great deal more problematic in some subject areas than others. What is important from a summative assessment perspective is that you are able to make your judgements with a degree of consistency. Again, subject-specific differences are likely to be noticed here. What is useful for the students is if 'the student comes to hold a concept of quality roughly similar to that held by the teacher' (Sadler, 1989, p121), and so shares your views of quality, an issue we shall return to in the section on formative assessment, and an important one for you, the teacher, to enact.

Effort and achievement

Our discussions on marking and grading so far have revealed that this is a difficult area, and one which although superficially self-evident, contains many underlying complexities. This is further compounded by the fact that another thing the seven original pieces of work in the reflective task above have in common is that they involve the students in engaging with the task, and producing a piece of work. For this reason many teachers also choose to indicate a grade for effort as well as achievement.

REFLECTIVE TASK

What is an effort grade?
How is it arrived at?
What does it mean to you, to the student, to the parents, to the head teacher?

Another common way for the teacher to summatively assess student work is via the use of a test. During the course of this chapter we will consider the form and nature of tests and testing, and discuss how these can be used in order to provide maximum information for both teacher and students. In order to do this effectively, we need to begin by thinking about what it is that will be subject to summative assessment.

Why use summative assessment?

Earlier on we asked the question 'what will happen to the results?' Another way of saying this is 'why are you assessing the students?' This question is a little more complex.

REFLECTIVE TASK

Can you think of summative assessment tests that you have observed or used while in school?
Why were they used?
What was their purpose?

It may be that you feel that the answer to the first of these questions is obvious. For example, the teacher wanted to know how much had been learned, and so gave the students a test. The test was used to find out how much of the topic had been learned, and the purpose was to tell the teacher which individuals had learned what. However, let us unpick this a little further. Think about what the test entailed. One issue which causes concern for teachers and students alike, is whether the test in question is a valid one or not. In Chapter 1 the notion of validity was discussed. As a trainee teacher you will want to make sure that the assessments which you use have some degree of validity. A common problem with validity is that use of English can get in the way of students' understanding. In a written description of the physics experiment, mentioned above as item 4 in our list of student tasks, it will be language which is used to describe the process. In the experiment itself it will be the actual doing of the experiment which forms the focus of attention. It is possible that there will be differences between the two. As Polanyi (1967, p4) observed, 'we can know more than we can tell'. While it is obviously impractical for students to always demonstrate practical knowledge in a practical way, nonetheless it seems likely that there will be differences between these two modes of assessment which have more to do with the nature of the assessment itself than with differences in student knowledge. The same student could score markedly differently on each of these assessments, and the difference will not be one of understanding, but of the use of English.

Macnamara's fallacy

This example from physics contains some obvious issues, which, as a reflective practitioner, you will have noted in advance of using these sorts of assessments. However, sometimes assessments can inadvertently prioritise something other than that which the teacher had intended. Sometimes, and this can relate to our discussion of quality above, that which is assessed is that which can be assessed, rather than that which is worth assessing. A classic version of this is known as Macnamara's fallacy, named after an American politician who argued that counting the number of war dead on both sides was a sensible thing to do. The general principles he expounded have since been placed into a much wider arena. Macnamara's fallacy runs like this:

> *The first step is to measure whatever can be easily measured. This is OK as far as it goes. The second step is to disregard that which can't easily be measured or to give it an arbitrary quantitative value. This is artificial and misleading. The third step is to presume that what can't be measured easily really isn't important. This is blindness. The fourth step is to say that what can't be easily measured really doesn't exist. This is suicide.*

(Handy, 1994, p219)

The danger for teachers is to measure whatever can be easily measured. In the case of the student writing a poem, it would be for the teacher to simply and mechanistically check whether each line-end rhymed. This would be a straightforward assessment to do, but would give no indication whatsoever as to the quality of ideas employed. In a music lesson, assessing whether a keyboard player used the right fingers for playing the melody they had composed would be another easy assessment to undertake from the teacher's perspective, but would totally ignore any original work which the student had put in to making up the piece of music. These might be extreme examples, but it is worthwhile bearing in mind the pitfalls of Macnamara's fallacy when you go about the business of devising assessment and assessment tasks.

Knowledge and summative assessment

This discussion concerning Macnamara's fallacy takes us into the area of knowledge. The knowledge evidenced by the student performing their own composition in music, painting their own picture in art, or writing a poem in English, are of a different nature to the sorts of knowledge required to undertake solving a page of equations or writing out a list of declensions of French verbs. We have already started, in earlier sections, to consider the nature of knowledge. As a teacher you already know that learning and knowledge are related. It is quite likely that one of the ways in which you will use summative assessments is as a means to discover what learning has taken place and what knowledge has been acquired during a teaching and learning episode. We discussed in Chapter 1 the differences between 'knowing that' and 'knowing how'. Another way of describing these different types of knowledge is to use the terminologies *declarative knowledge* and *procedural knowledge*. Declarative knowledge is knowledge which, literally, can be declared, in other words spoken about and said out loud. Procedural knowledge relates to knowing how to undertake a task, and normally has connotations of doing about it, in other words it relates to the notion of Ryle's (1949) we discussed earlier, that of knowing how. These distinctions of knowledge are important, not only from a philosophical perspective, but from the practical perspective of what is going on in your classroom.

REFLECTIVE TASK

Think about your subject area. Can you distinguish between types of knowledge which could be considered declarative, and those which could be considered as procedural?

So having thought about these different types of knowledge, what you will want to do now is to consider the teaching and learning which are appropriate to them. In Chapter 1 we considered the case of a PE teacher inappropriately assessing her students' javelin skills by the use of an essay. How will you avoid falling into this trap? How will you make sure your assessments are fit for purpose?

Answers to these issues are obviously going to depend on your specialist subject, but it seems likely that you will want to assess procedural knowledge in a fashion which allows for knowledge of procedures to be employed.

PRACTICAL TASK PRACTICAL TASK PRACTICAL TASK PRACTICAL TASK PRACTICAL TASK

When you are next observing a lesson given by an experienced teacher, try to find out how they deal with different sorts of knowledge, how they assess the students, and how they reflect on the effectiveness of their own teaching.

RESEARCH SUMMARY RESEARCH SUMMARY RESEARCH SUMMARY RESEARCH SUMMARY

Another way of considering the nature of knowledge has been described by Sfard (1998), in her discussion concerning metaphors for learning. The two metaphors that she employs are those of *acquisition* and *participation*. In the acquisition metaphor, knowledge is treated as a commodity and, rather in the way that when you go round a supermarket you select items off the shelves to put in your trolley, this is more or less how knowledge can be treated. In the participation metaphor, knowledge is considered as something in which the learner takes part. As she puts it:

> ... *learning a subject is now conceived of as a process of becoming a member of a certain community. This entails, above all, the ability to communicate in the language of this community and act according to its particular norms ... While the learners are newcomers ... the teachers are the preservers of its continuity.*

> (Sfard, 1998, p6)

This way of looking at knowledge, although having obvious links with Vygotsky's notion of the zone of proximal development, is not solely about the social construction of learning. In her article, Sfard warns against relying too heavily on just one of these metaphors.

These different views of knowledge will hopefully have set you thinking about what it is which is going on in your classroom. Considering Sfard's notion of metaphors may lead you to think about the types of knowledge which your subject requires. So, a French conversation requires a number of different types of knowledge; the students need a grammar, and knowledge of words, they need to be familiar with the motions of turn-taking which conversation requires, and they need to be thinking about what the respondent says to them. For the teacher, observing a conversation between two students requires them to consider which aspects of their work the students are going to need help with. If homework from this lesson is to write up the conversation, then a different set of skills will be overlaid on top of the original. Assessment of this, which involves writing, will, of necessity, be different from the original practical application of speaking.

REFLECTIVE TASK

Try to think of examples similar to that of the French lesson which would apply in your subject area. How can you deal with minimising the effects of this?

Certification

A common use for summative assessment is to provide certification of achievement, often by the employment of an externally validated testing regime. Many of these certifications are considered to be assessments which 'matter', and are consequently referred to as being 'high-stakes' assessments. These include GCSE, AS and A2 examinations. Your role in these high-stakes assessments is often to interpret the published examination specification, and then deconstruct it into a learning programme for your students.

Starting from a published summative assessment plan

The closer one gets to the students and their learning, the more closely defined targets will be. When one deals with the performance of cohorts or populations, the more coarsely defined targets will be.

(Blanchard, 2003, p262)

This quotation from Blanchard leads us into a consideration of teaching and learning for examination groups. As a beginning teacher your concerns, as we have noted, are likely to be grounded in the day-to-day learning of your classes. However, when you teach examination groups, you will be steering the students in your care towards an assessment system which is, depending on the subject and level involved, dictated by external agencies. This requires a slightly different approach from one where you have legislated for the learning and the assessment integrally. The targets for your students, as Blanchard notes, will be based on your knowledge of them as individual learners; the targets set by the examination will have been published with a much wider view in mind. One of the tasks that you will have to do as a teacher is to think about how you can move from externally published examination specifications towards producing units of work and schemes of learning based upon them. This task can take a variety of forms, and will, to a greater or lesser extent, be determined by what assistance you are given by the examination boards themselves in the form of supporting materials. You will also have the help of more experienced colleagues in the school and department.

As there will be a variety of examination specifications which readers of this book will be following, we are only able to talk in general terms about this matter. It will then be up to you to place this into the overlapping contexts of your specialist teaching subject, in your school, with your students, and the resources at your disposal.

PRACTICAL TASK PRACTICAL TASK PRACTICAL TASK PRACTICAL TASK PRACTICAL TASK

Look at a range of current examination specifications for your subject. What proportion of grades in each of them is devoted to coursework, and what to final examination?

There are two main issues to consider here: coursework and final examinable component. The way you prepare to teach each of these will differ.

Coursework

The matter of coursework has become one of a political 'hot potato' recently, with studies and commentators raising issues of gender inequality, help from parents, perceived ease of different subject areas, and so on. For your purposes you need to deal with the reality of coursework as it will be taught and learned, and so we will sidestep these issues, and move to considering your actions.

Coursework entails a period of protracted work by the student, realised over time, and then assessed at a specific point.

PRACTICAL TASK PRACTICAL TASK PRACTICAL TASK PRACTICAL TASK PRACTICAL TASK

Who assesses the coursework in your subject? Is it you, is it your department? Is it sent off to an external marker?

If coursework is to be assessed by you, it is likely that you will need to keep some record of what happens over time. If it is to be assessed externally, then you may have to provide some evidence of development, and to be able to comment on how progression has happened over time. In Chapter 1 we discussed the notion of assessment being located within a view of teaching learning. In the case of working from examination specifications, the published assessment criteria will be your starting point, and you will then derive your own assessment criteria from these. Figure 3.2 shows this altered emphasis.

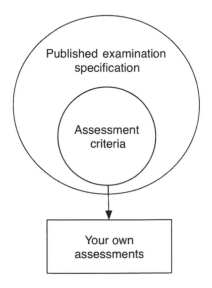

Figure 3.2 From examination specification to your own assessments

This way of working needs a slight difference of approach from planning for learning when you are in control of the overall learning outcomes, as you will need to ensure that you are able to undertake sequential planning for learning from the information you are given from the examination boards. An important point here is the notion of *sequential* planning for assessment. The exam specification is likely to be concerned with *terminal assessment*, that which the students will be doing at the end of their course. You, on the other hand, need to be aware of the journey towards this, hence your need to sequence the route which the students will follow to arrive at this desired endpoint.

Although the overall summative assessment at the end of a 'high-stakes' assessment course, such as GCSE, involves preparing the students for this, it does not mean that you have recourse solely to summative criteria as you prepare the students for their exams. You are interpreting the published summative criteria for the end of a learning period; in the case of GCSE this is normally two years. The general principles of assessment for learning, and all of the other examples of good practice we discuss in this book, can, and should, be applied here too.

Conclusion

Having considered views of knowledge and types of learning in Chapter 2, we can see that summative assessment has a number of uses in documenting achievement. It is important to realise, however, that because by its very nature summative assessment looks back on achievement, what it is troublesome to use it for is to develop future learning. In other words, how to work out what needs to be done next, what could be done to improve performance or achievement, or what aspects of learning would benefit from intervention. It is possible to use summative assessment in a formative fashion, and this is a topic we shall return to after we have considered what is going on in formative assessment itself in Chapter 4.

Summative assessment is a major and important part of the teacher's day-to-day work in the classroom, and it is likely that you will be employing summative assessment techniques in many aspects of your teaching. In this chapter we have considered a number of aspects of summative assessment. We have thought about the ways in which summative assessment can be used to look back on learning, document achievement, and be used as evidence of learning. We have looked at issues concerned with marking and grading, and we have discussed notions of fitness for purpose. Summative assessment plays an important role in the public face of the school, and it is student grades publicly displayed which form the basis of examination league tables. As a certification measure summative assessment will play an important part in your life as a teacher, and you will develop your own strategies and techniques for day-to-day employment in your classroom.

A SUMMARY OF **KEY POINTS**

In this chapter you have:
> **learned about summative assessment;**
> **thought about the uses and purposes of marking and grading;**
> **reflected on what quality is in your subject area and ...**
> **... how you can assess it;**
> **learned about Macnamara's fallacy, and the danger of simply assessing that which is easy to assess, and missing that which is worth assessing;**

> reflected on the certification role of summative assessment;
> considered how different types of knowledge – knowing how and knowing that – require different types of assessment.

REFERENCES REFERENCES **REFERENCES** REFERENCES **REFERENCES** REFERENCES

Blanchard, J. (2003) Targets, assessment for learning, and whole-school improvement. *Cambridge Journal of Education,* 33(2): 257–71.

Handy, C.B. (1994) *The empty raincoat*. London: Hutchinson.

Pirsig, R. (1974) *Zen and the art of motorcycle maintenance*. London: Vintage.

Polanyi, M. (1967) *The tacit dimension*. London: Routledge & Kegan Paul.

Ryle, G. (1949) *The concept of mind*. London: Penguin Books.

Sadler, D. (1989) Formative assessment and the design of instructional systems. *Instructional Science,* 18: 119–44.

Sfard, A. (1998) On two metaphors for learning and the dangers of choosing just one. *Educational Researcher,* 27(2): 4–13.

FURTHER READING FURTHER READING **FURTHER READING** FURTHER READING

Brooks, V. (2002) *Assessment in secondary schools: the new teacher's guide to monitoring, assessment, recording, reporting and accountability*. Buckingham: Open University Press.

Gipps, C. and Murphy, P. (1994) *A fair test?: Assessment, achievement and equity*. Buckingham: Open University Press.

Youens, B. (2005) External examinations and assessment, in Capel, S., Leask, M. and Turner, T. (eds) *Learning to teach in the secondary school.* London: RoutledgeFalmer.

4
Formative assessment

Introduction

Appropriate use of formative assessment holds the potential for helping to raise standards in schools, and, as such, a number of aspects of it have featured in a several recent governmental and educational initiatives. You will doubtless have become aware of its importance in teaching and learning from professional studies, other taught sessions, and your background reading during your course of initial teacher education.

In educational parlance 'formative assessment' and 'assessment for learning' have come to be synonymous. In some publications you will find references to the former, and in others to the latter. For the purposes of this book, we will be using the terms interchangeably. Sometimes this difference in usage is contextual, and at other times it is derived from a consideration of textual materials.

We have already seen in earlier chapters of this book how formative assessment differs from summative assessment in that it uses information from the present in order to look forward to the future. What this means for you is that formative assessment of learning is, and should be, a major part of your everyday teaching. But what does this involve in practice? What is it that you should be doing when engaging in formative assessment?

REFLECTIVE TASK

From what you know already, what do you believe that doing formative assessment in the classroom entails?

There are likely to have been a number of different answers to this question, so in order to clarify and focus our thinking, let us turn to one of the major publications from the early days of formative assessment research, *Inside the Black Box* (Black and Wiliam, 1998b). In this publication Black and Wiliam suggest that there are four areas involved in formative assessment:

- **questioning;**
- **feedback;**
- **sharing criteria;**
- **self assessment.**

Since then, a fifth area has often been added, that of peer assessment; sometimes linked with self-assessment, and sometimes treated as a topic in its own right.

You will remember from earlier chapters that we discussed how historically assessment and instruction had been viewed as being 'curiously separate' from each other. The areas suggested by Black and Wiliam are not aspects of assessment separate from teaching, but are inherently bound up with teaching and learning processes. We shall now consider each of them in turn.

Questioning

Research has shown that a considerable proportion of teacher time in lessons involves asking questions.

REFLECTIVE TASK

Think about the most recent lesson you taught. Do you have any idea how many questions you asked? Had you planned for any of them in advance? What sort of questions are there? What sort of answers were you looking for?

Unless you wrote a script for your lesson, it is unlikely that you will remember exactly how many questions you asked. It may be that you had planned for some of them in advance, and so will remember these. Other questions will have formed part of everyday conversational dialogues between you and your students.

Open and closed questions

When discussing different types of question, it is customary to refer to them as being one of two types.

- **Closed questions. These are questions which essentially have only one answer, generally right or wrong, e.g. 'What is the capital of France?'; 'Who wrote *Bleak House*?'**
- **Open questions. These are questions which require slightly more by way of an answer. For some there can be more than one answer, for others an extended answer is required, for others some element of personal engagement might be needed, e.g. 'What is the best way to travel from London to Edinburgh?' 'What was the state of religious toleration under Queen Elizabeth I?' 'What do you feel about the current political situation in Ecuador?'**

Classroom research has revealed that teachers ask a far greater number of closed questions than open questions. This can sometimes be problematic, as closed questions generally require single-word or very short answers and can privilege the students who have this information at their fingertips. Open questions require slightly more by way of cognitive engagement before the answerer is able to give a considered response. This is not to say that one type of question is 'better' than the other, but it may well be that repeated use of closed questions will not facilitate all of the students having equal access to answering them; neither will it allow the students to progress to the more advanced thinking necessary to develop longer answers.

Wait time

While on the topic of closed questions, have you thought about how much time you give the students before you accept answers from them? Do you start to ask a question and then find that a number of students already have their hands up and are 'straining at the leash' in order to be first to answer, whereas others seldom, if ever, participate in the rapid patter of quick-fire closed questioning sessions? If this is the case then the notion of wait time may be useful for you.

RESEARCH SUMMARY RESEARCH SUMMARY **RESEARCH SUMMARY** RESEARCH SUMMARY

Wait time

The concept of 'wait time' as something which should be taken seriously in allowing students time to answer questions posed by teachers in classrooms was discussed by Mary Budd Rowe (Rowe, 1974). In her research she found that wait time periods between teacher question and students answering rarely exceeded 1.5 seconds. She also discovered that when this wait time was doubled to 3 seconds a number of benefits accrued. These included:

- **the length and correctness of the answers given increased;**
- **the number of people who did not know the answer decreased;**
- **the number of students who elected to answer increased.**

Three seconds is not a very long time, although it might seem odd waiting in silence and not allowing students to put their hands up until this time has elapsed. However, as Mary Budd Rowe found out, it may well be worth you trying this technique in order to increase students' thinking time as well as enhance the quality of responses that you get.

PRACTICAL TASK PRACTICAL TASK PRACTICAL TASK PRACTICAL TASK PRACTICAL TASK

Wait time

Next time you ask a question, allow more time before you accept an answer. You can tell the students you are doing this, and say something like 'I shall wait five seconds before anybody puts their hands up'.

But what about open-ended questions? What sorts of questions are you asking here? Is there anything you can do to develop your questioning technique? One of the ways in which researchers have addressed this issue is to be found in the use of Bloom's taxonomy (Bloom, 1956). This is by no means the only way in which questioning can be considered, but it does have the advantage of being a tried-and-tested device, and, as it has figured in a number of recent governmental initiatives, is one with which teachers in schools are likely to have some familiarity.

Bloom's taxonomy

Bloom's *taxonomy of educational objectives of the cognitive domain* was first published in the 1950s and resulted from Bloom and his fellow researchers categorising and classifying questions which were commonly asked in educational settings. A diagrammatic representation of Bloom's taxonomy is to be found in Figure 4.1.

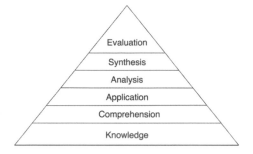

Figure 4.1 Bloom's taxonomy

The picture in Figure 4.1 is intended to show a progression from the bottom of the pyramid, knowledge, to the top, evaluation. The first three levels are generally considered to be concerned with lower-order thinking, the top three levels with higher-order thinking.

So, if some types of thinking can be classified as being of a higher order than others, how can you as a classroom teacher decide on the most appropriate questioning strategy to foster different levels of thinking in your classroom? To answer this question, and make it directly applicable for you, let us consider what forming questions to address each of the six levels of Bloom's taxonomy might look like.

Knowledge
Knowledge questions are ones which you can ask to find out what is known by the students. These will often tend to be closed questions which involve recall of subject matter, knowledge of specific facts, and learned responses and behaviours.

Comprehension
Comprehension questions involve moving beyond knowing, towards understanding. They include questions which are designed to discover whether the students have grasped the meaning of something, or can show that they can apply knowledge in a different context.

Application
Application questions involve using information in order to solve problems, to use ideas in new and different situations, and to be able to demonstrate that the students are able to apply existing skills and knowledge. This category includes questions designed to find out whether students can apply theoretical knowledge across a range of situations.

Analysis
Questioning for analysis involves the students being able to demonstrate that they are able to detect how something has been formed, or account what is going on in an event. It involves them in recognition, pattern spotting, and revealing their understanding of structure. Questioning in this category can also involve comparison, of being able to classify a new object by applying existing knowledge, and being able to look beyond the surface to uncover hidden or inferred meanings.

Synthesis

Questioning for synthesis involves students in combining knowledge from different areas, and being able to generalise from series of facts. It also involves creating new meanings from extant knowledge, and being able to arrive at a logical conclusion.

Evaluation

Evaluation is the highest order in Bloom's taxonomy, and involves students in being able to place relative value on things. It can also involve them in comparing and discriminating between different ideas, concepts or objects. It may also involve them in becoming aware of value judgements and of the differences between opinions and facts.

We asked you above whether you had planned for the questions which you were asking in your classroom. In questioning planning for assessment for learning it is helpful for you to have some questions which you have prepared in advance. A useful way of doing this is to prepare your questions from given stems, which start the question off for you, and which you then complete with material appropriate to your context. Table 4.1 gives a list of possible question stems for you to adapt with your classes.

Table 4.1: Question stems

Knowledge	What is... Can you remember... What happened when... In what year was... What does that add up to...
Comprehension	Explain what you mean by... Can you show me an example where you... What is going on here... Can you show me how you are able to... Are you able to put that in your own words...
Application	How will you do this... Can you think of another example of... Can you show me an instance where... How will you carry out...
Analysis	How is this similar to... Can you compare that with... How can you tell the difference between that and... What events led up to that goal... What was the problem with... Can you distinguish between that and... Are you able to describe how you...
Synthesis	What would happen if you were to put your ideas together with hers... What would happen if you changed that bit where... How could you do this differently... Could you put those ideas into your song...
Evaluation	What was successful about... What changes might you make... Can you justify why... How do you feel about... Why do you think that... Would it be a good thing if...

Using the question stems from Table 4.1, think about a lesson you will be teaching soon, and prepare a series of questions from knowledge through to evaluation.

However, using questioning as an assessment for learning activity involves more than just asking good questions. You also need to listen to the answers, pay attention to, and act upon, what the students tell you. Questioning by itself might not tell you anything – it is what you do with the answers that becomes important.

Thinking about this leads us towards the next area of formative assessment which we shall consider, that of feedback.

Feedback

Giving feedback to students involves more than simply telling them what it is that they are doing wrong. Giving feedback involves a dialogue between teacher and students. It focuses, as Figure 4.2 shows, on discussing student work in the present in order to positively influence student achievement in the future.

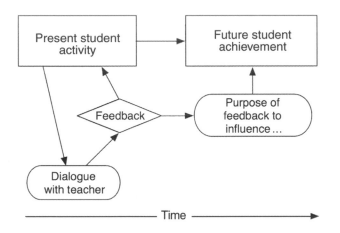

Figure 4.2 Feedback

Figure 4.2 shows that discussing student activity and giving feedback in the immediate here and now will have a positive effect on student learning. The feedback given in this way also has an effect on future student achievement. This specific type of feedback is often known as feedforward.

Feedforward

We have discussed how you will be having dialogues with your students focusing on helping them with their current work, and giving them feedback to help them with this. It is also possible to give a specifically targeted form of feedback which is designed to help the students in work they will be doing in the future, in other words *feedforward*. Figure 4.3 re-draws Figure 4.2 to take account of this.

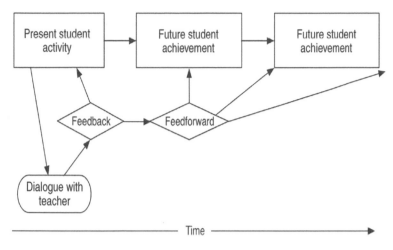

Figure 4.3 Feedforward

What is happening in feedforward is that you are using information deriving from your knowledge of where the students are now in order to make judgements and have discussions about where the students should be next. This is an important part of the work of a teacher. You will need to have a clear view of where the students' learning should be heading. An important point for you to remember is that what the students are doing now will become prior learning for the next programme of study or unit of work. This is why it helps to have a clear and progressional view of the overall learning which students will be doing in their subject lessons.

Personalising feedback

It is important in our discussions on feedback for you to ensure you distinguish between *teaching* and *learning*. Giving feedback involves individualising and personalising learning so that the students know specifically what they need to do in order to improve. The place of feedback in a learning episode is likely to occur during the central phase of a lesson. Often teachers begin with a starter activity, then move to a period of whole-class instruction or action, sometimes working on a more individual basis, before heading towards a plenary at the end of the lesson. It is most likely to be during individual learning opportunities that you will have the chance to engage in constructive dialogue with your students. But what sorts of feedback are appropriate, and what sorts of things should you be saying?

In a section such as this on formative assessment it is patently appropriate that we will be recommending that your feedback should be that, i.e. formative. Formative feedback informs the student with regard to what they should be doing next in order to improve. This is rather different in kind from judgemental feedback which simply emphasises deficiencies in student performance. What we as teachers should be interested in is positive, supportive, personalised comments which derive from the specific situation of learners.

TEACHING EXAMPLE
English
In an English lesson a group of students were working together to write a short story on a horror theme, involving night-time, woods, and a girl walking alone. They had begun their story, and the teacher was moving from group to group giving assistance, engaging in

---

dialogue, and giving feedback. She listened to each group's story so far, and then used questioning to draw out understandings of the work which the students had been doing. The feedback which she gave them was based very firmly on their individual stories; she did not try to draw out generalisations, or speak to the whole class. Instead she was very focused on making her comments appropriate to the work of the group she was talking to. One of her concerns was with the story not becoming gory, but of maintaining an atmosphere of unspoken and unforeseen fear. Her feedback grew out of these concerns, and by acting on her responses the students were able to develop their stories in an appropriate fashion.

Making feedback constructive

To be worthwhile, feedback needs to involve contributions from all parties involved in a learning exchange. What it is not is a teacher monologue. A useful way of thinking about this is to be found in the notion of an IRF cycle (Brooks, 2002, p55; Torrance and Pryor, 1998, p17). An IRF cycle involves three stages.

- **Initiation: this is where the teacher asks questions.**
- **Responses: here the students reply.**
- **Feedback: the teacher reacts to the responses of the students.**

This way of working involves the feedback being targeted towards helping students know what it is they need to do in order to improve. According to the Assessment Reform Group, in order to do this:

> *Learners need information and guidance in order to plan the next steps in their learning. Teachers should: pinpoint the learner's strengths and advise on how to develop them; be clear and constructive about any weaknesses and how they might be addressed; provide opportunities for learners to improve upon their work.*
>
> (Assessment Reform Group, 2002)

This emphasis on being constructive is important. You need to be aware that all assessments are likely to carry some form of emotional impact. Only pointing out defects is not likely to do anything for your students' self-esteem. Obviously you are looking for improvement, but improvement is a positive attribute, and you need to emphasise this, even though you may think that their work so far involves a deficit of some kind. Being negative at this juncture might jeopardise the value of any subsequent positive comments which you make. Torrance and Pryor (1998, p169) observed that in some cases teachers' use of IRF produced 'negative consequences for both learning and social development'. So in order to counter this, feedback should, as the ARG point out, be 'sensitive and constructive'.

Process and product

You are likely to have observed during your time in schools that there is some pressure on teachers and students to achieve high levels, marks and grades in summative assessments. It is inevitable that some of this pressure will rub off on you as a beginning teacher. In a formative assessment situation it is important to consider that there is a distinction in many examples of student learning between the *process* of learning, and the *product* which results from it. In summative assessment it is often the product which is the focus of attention, the process by which that product was achieved is in many cases of little or no interest.

BEELECLIAE 1V2K
REFLECTIVE TASK

Think of an example of something which you can do. Maybe you can play the piano, maybe you can tap dance, maybe you can grow prize marrows, maybe you play football. Whatever it is, think about it, and try to separate the process of learning which you went through in order to 'do', from the product, the 'doing', which results.

Let us take the first of these examples, playing the piano. A common way to assess progress in piano playing is via the use of graded examinations. Maybe you have done some of these yourself. What happens in these is that the young pianist learns a number of pieces of music, goes to an examination centre, and plays them to an examiner. Depending on how well (or not) they play them will determine whether or not they pass the examination. The process which they went through to get to this stage, the many hours of lessons and practice count for nothing; everything depends on performance on the day, the product.

However, if you are the piano teacher you want your student to get better, and you will be offering assistive comments, showing them how to play difficult passages, and offering tips on performance. In other words, the concern of the piano teacher is with both process, the ways in which the student is learning, and product, performance of the piece which results from learning. The comments made during learning will involve positive supportive feedback; this is formative assessment in action. The piano teacher will know what a good performance sounds like, and will be able to model this to their students. The students will gain an idea of what good-quality piano playing sounds like, and will endeavour to emulate this in their own music-making. The task for you is to transfer this model to your own lessons and classes. To do this you need to know what good performance in your subject involves, to be able to model this to your students, and to be able to share with them what it means to improve.

Formative feedback instead of grading

It is not only during the course of a lesson that you are likely to want to give feedback. When students have completed a piece of work, whatever that might mean in your subject, it is likely in many cases that some form of formalised assessment process is expected. This could be a point at which marking and grading take place. Here you may wish to think about what it is that you do when undertake this task.

BEELECLIAE 1V2K
REFLECTIVE TASK

What forms can a piece of work take in your subject?
What will you do to mark and grade it?
Will you write comments?
Will you write a grade?
Will you do both?

What a piece of work will look like in your subject can vary enormously, even within a single subject. You may well have come up with a list of things, ranging from tasks and practical activities, to written work and essays. How you mark it might depend on purpose. We will look further at this in later sections, but for the moment let us think about the notion of giving formative feedback instead of grading. If you write (or speak) comments about a piece of work, then these will be matters which you deem important, and can help clarify understandings, develop arguments, point out errors, suggest ways forward, or many other possibilities. If, as well as this, you give a grade, then research has shown that it is the grade, the mark given, which is looked at first; only after this are comments looked at, and then, in many cases, only cursorily. Many students appear to think to themselves things along the lines of , 'I got a B minus (or level 4, or seven out of ten, or whatever), that's good enough'. The comments are not important to this process.

No grades, comment-only feedback
What formative assessment research has investigated is the notion of not giving grades to the students, only comments. In many cases the teachers were still allotting grades, but only recording them in their mark books, not sharing them with the students, or making them public. What has happened where this has been tried is that, in many cases, students pay attention to the comments they have been given, the formative feedback, and make adjustments accordingly.

PRACTICAL TASK PRACTICAL TASK PRACTICAL TASK PRACTICAL TASK PRACTICAL TASK

Discuss with your mentor whether you could try not giving grades for a piece of work where you normally would. What are the mentor's feelings and thoughts on this? Is this part of their practice? What do they think might happen if it was introduced where it had not existed before? To work effectively this probably needs to be built in to medium- and long-term planning. If this task proves difficult during your teacher training year, perhaps you can try it out when you are an NQT.

Sharing criteria

It is quite normal in schools nowadays to find learning objectives written on the board at the beginning of the lesson. It may well be the case in your school placements that you are encouraged to do this by your mentors and tutors.

REFLECTIVE TASK

Think back to the most recent occasion you wrote lesson or learning objectives on the board in your classroom. Now, think very carefully about them. What were they about? Were they:

a) learning objectives in the true sense, and described briefly the learning which was to take place, or...

b) task objectives, in that they described what the students were going to do?

When you were writing these objectives on the board, did you have a clear idea as to what a successful outcome would be from this lesson? Did you share this with the students?

Knowing what a good outcome is from a lesson is clearly important for you as a teacher and it is likely to be equally important for the students. In 'curiously separate' assessment practices it is possible that the students do not know what the assessment criteria are to which they will be subject. In the previous chapter on summative assessment we considered the notion of quality, and observed how Sadler (1989) had noted that it was important for students 'to hold a concept of quality roughly similar to that held by the teacher'. This is what it means to share criteria with the students. The students need to understand what a good piece of work will entail. In order for them to do this, it may seem obvious to say, but you as the teacher will need an understanding of what a good-quality piece of work will involve. You may meet teachers who say to you 'I don't need a mark scheme, I just know what I'm looking for', but this will not help the students, nor will it help you in your development as a professional teacher. What you need to be able to articulate is what learning you expect to take place in your lesson, and then use assessment to:

- **find out what learning has taken place;**
- **ascertain to what degree in various students learning has occurred;**
- **evaluate the efficacy of your teaching;**
- **work out where next to go with student learning;**
- **adjust your teaching strategy accordingly.**

To be able to do this you need to know with some degree of precision what learning you hoped would happen, what learning might have taken place serendipitously, what learning has happened, and whether there are any gaps or omissions in the students' learning. This takes us towards a discussion of learning outcomes, of planning for learning, and of using assessment to help in this process, and it is to these areas that we shall now turn.

Learning outcomes and assessment criteria

For beginning teachers the links between learning outcomes and assessment criteria cannot be overstated. Clearly written learning outcomes can either become their own assessment criteria, or will lead in a linear fashion to crafting assessment criteria from them. What this means for you in practice is that you have to spend some time in carefully planning your learning outcomes. In addition you are likely to be required to differentiate your learning outcomes. Let us take a three-part differentiation of learning outcomes into 'all', 'most' and 'some'. In this not uncommon form of differentiation of learning outcomes, 'all' refers to the base level of achievement; this is what everyone in the class will learn. 'Most' students will go beyond this base level, and will learn more, or at a higher level. 'Some' will go on further than this, and will be in need of deeper learning, or extensions in terms of skills, concepts, tasks or activities.

Doing and learning

This tripartite division, all–most–some, focuses your thinking on to what it is specifically that you want the students to learn. A common trap that beginning teachers fall into is to confuse *doing* with *learning*. In other words, task outcomes are privileged over learning outcomes. You will doubtless discover many teachers who say 'this is a nice activity, why don't you try it with your classes?'. Your aim in these situations is to uncover what the learning is in the task in question. You may find that although it is a perfectly acceptable activity, the students learn little or nothing by undertaking it. To counter this, what you need to be doing at this early stage of your teaching career is really thinking very carefully about what learning is. This is a point which we shall revisit in Chapter 5.

REFLECTIVE TASK

Write a learning outcome now for a lesson you will teach fairly soon where the learning outcomes are divided like this:

all – something which everyone in the class will be able to learn;
most – something which a majority of students in the class will be able to learn;
some – something which a few of the students in the class will go on to learn.

Many units of work and lesson plans which you will need to write have to cover a number of aspects of study. You will need to plan for and write separate learning outcomes for each of these areas.

TEACHING EXAMPLE
Maths

In the National Curriculum, knowledge skills and understanding in mathematics appear under three headings: number and algebra; shape, space and measures; and handling data. In your differentiated learning outcomes it is likely that you will have to formulate all–most–some outcomes for each of these.

Assessment criteria do not solely apply to pieces of written work. Art teachers will know what they are looking for in a visual response, music teachers in an auditory one, dance teachers in movement, and so on, depending on your specialism.

Planning to integrate assessment within learning

In order to take this a stage further, let us work through an example of planning for a piece of work which will involve sharing assessment criteria with students. Figure 4.4 takes you through a number of stages in planning for a unit of work, or for an individual lesson within the unit. Notice especially the two boxes in bold type, 'what are the learning outcomes' and 'what are the assessment criteria': these show clearly the linkages that we have been talking about.

The planning process begins, logically enough, with you thinking about what it is that you want the students to learn. If you are on teaching practice, it may be that you are being asked to fit into an existing unit of work or programme of study. In this case you will need to find out what prior learning the students have already, as this is an obviously important part of contextualising learning.

How you will structure learning, and whether this will involve the whole class, small groups, or individual students, will obviously depend on the specific aspect of the subject which you are teaching, and the learning and supporting activities which you have planned for.

Writing learning outcomes
Writing succinct learning outcomes forms the next, and possibly most important, part of the planning process. We have already discussed learning outcomes, but at this stage it is worthwhile to point out that many trainee teachers, and, in fact, many experienced teachers, find this the least straightforward part of planning. Writing good learning outcomes takes practice, but it is most worthwhile, as it is from these learning outcomes that the whole thrust of the programme of study, unit of work or individual lesson plan will take shape. As we noted above, and will return to in later chapters, good learning outcomes can be reapplied as assessment criteria.

Having written your assessment criteria derived from your learning outcomes, you are likely to want to translate these into 'student speak'. At this point a significant assessment for

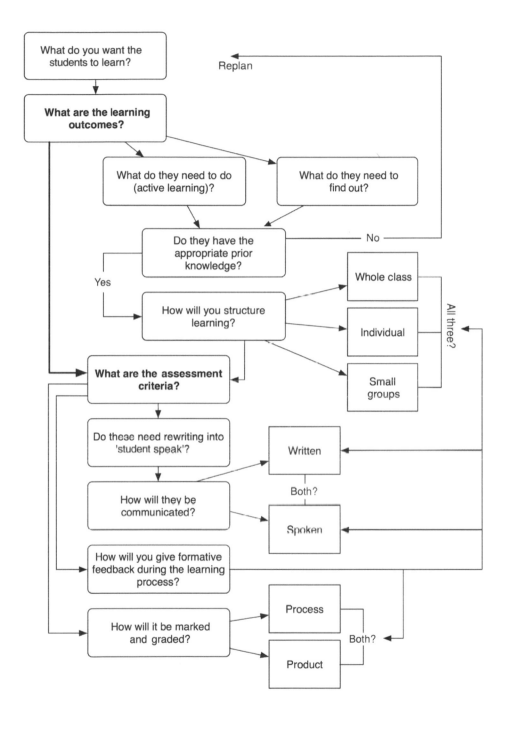

Figure 4.4 Formative assessment planning

learning decision needs to take place. We have seen how many teachers write learning outcomes, or lesson objectives, on the board at the start of the lesson. For practical purposes these will need to be short, precise and to the point. What you may find it appropriate to do is to take time to explain these in a discussion with the students. In this case the shortened version written up on the board acts as an *aide-mémoire* for the students, rather than simply being written on the board and then ignored for the remainder of the lesson.

Sharing assessment criteria

The learning outcomes you have written are likely to be not the only judgements you will be making during the course of the lesson. You will probably ask the students to do something, and it is here that the notion of sharing criteria becomes important. What many teachers have found helpful is to say to the students 'what I am looking for is people who can. . .', or 'what a successful piece of work will have, is. . .', or some variation on this depending on your context. In a very simple and straightforward way this gives the students some ownership over their role in meeting the success criteria for the work the students are doing.

TEACHING EXAMPLE

English

An English teacher wanted to develop punctuation with one of her Year 7 classes. Rather than do this out of context, she approached it in collaboration with the drama teacher, and they worked jointly on the students writing and acting out short scenarios of school life. The focus in drama was on drama-specific learning, while the focus in English was writing speech with punctuation. This collaboration was fruitful for both parties.

In this teaching example the drama teacher in her lessons was concerned with speaking, action, movement and emotional content. In the English lesson, the concern shifted to one of notation, but done so in a real context. As the students worked in small groups on writing out their scenarios, the English teacher moved among them, discussed what they were doing, gave them individual targeted feedback which personalised the learning experience for them, and shared with them the fact that she was looking for punctuation, and this was the area of concern for her. This simple and straightforward collaboration can be repeated across many subject areas, and might not need to involve interdepartmental working. It is entirely possible for you to set up a situation where the learning is contextualised within a task, authentic or otherwise, and you give formative feedback to the students as they are working.

Giving formative feedback

We now move to the box in Figure 4.4 which asks you to think about how you will give formative feedback during the learning process. Will this be to individuals, small groups, or the whole class, or a combination of these? The answer to this will depend, to a large extent, on how you have set up the learning. There may be things which you need to share with the class as a whole that you uncover from your conversations with students, rather than say the same thing 30 times to 30 different students. It is obviously a more sensible use of time to say this once to the whole class. There may be things which you find out from your dialogues that some groups have not quite got the hang of. In this case you will want to give feedback to them with regard to this issue. For some individuals, you may want to spend a few minutes dealing with their personalised learning agendas. Managing the multiple simultaneity of complex classroom interactions is a part of the learning process for you as a teacher, and is likely to require some practice, and possibly the help of a more experienced mentor.

Learning process and outcomes

The final part of figure 4.4 asks you to consider how the work the students have done will be marked and graded. Indeed, as we discussed above, in some cases you may not wish to share this with the students, and give formative feedback only, either in written or spoken form.

We have already commented on differences between the process of learning, and the ensuing learning outcomes. Sharing criteria, remember 'what I am looking for is students who can...', also involves process. Some research has shown that students need to be steered away from thinking that what teachers look for is results, and that how these are arrived at does not matter. This sort of thinking needs to be addressed, and sharing criteria for the process of activities is a good way of achieving this. To help emphasise this, the 'what I am looking for is students who can...' phrase needs emphasising over 'what I am looking for is students who have done...', and it is worth spending some time explaining this to the class.

The idea of students taking responsibility for their own learning takes us to another of the areas we listed at the start of this chapter, that of peer and self-assessment.

Peer and self-assessment

Peer assessment often goes hand-in-hand with self-assessment. Put simply, peer assessment involves students assessing the work of other students, their peers; while self-assessment involves each individual in a consideration of their own work. Unlike many of the other aspects of assessment we have discussed so far, trainee and beginning teachers sometimes have problems with the notions and practices of peer and self-assessment when used with school students. In addition, many established practitioners also struggle with this, so do not worry if you see very little evidence of it on your school placements, this does not mean it is not a worthwhile thing to do.

When Black and Wiliam were investigating formative assessment in classrooms, one of the studies they reported on was from Portuguese maths teachers, where:

> *The focus of the assessment work was on regular – mainly daily – self assessment by the students. This involved teaching them to understand both the learning objectives and the assessment criteria, giving them opportunity to choose learning tasks and using tasks which gave them scope to assess their own learning outcomes.*

> (Black and Wiliam, 1998a, p10)

This study showed that involving students in thinking about learning objectives and assessment criteria showed a statistically significant difference, where the mean gain made by the group concerned was almost twice that of the control group. Clearly this would be an impressive feat to reproduce in your classroom. But for you as a trainee or beginning teacher, peer and self-assessment are not easily transferable into your lessons. To use effective techniques requires some preparatory work to be done with the students before you and they can begin to put it into action.

Before we move on to consider how you can introduce peer and self-assessment techniques in your lessons, let us think about why this might be a good thing to do.

There are many possible answers to this question, but they all reduce to issues of learning. If students do not realise how their learning can be improved, and importantly, what specifically they need to do to be able to improve it, then they will not get better. As James observes:

> If students are to learn from their own performance in order to improve, they need to be able to assess and evaluate their actual *performance against standards. They need to identify any gaps between actual and desired levels and they need to be able to work out why those gaps have occurred. Then, they need to identify the strategies that they might use to close the gap and meet the standard on another occasion. This is a complex activity but it has to be done by the students because it is they who are the learners and they need to internalise the process. Learning cannot be done* for *them by the teachers.*

> (James, 1998, p176)

You will probably hear teachers in the staffroom say things like 'I don't why they haven't learned it, I've taught it to them a thousand times'; when you do it is helpful to remember the 'mantra' from earlier in this book: 'Teaching ≠ Learning'. James's point is pertinent here: you, the teacher, cannot do the learning for your students. The purpose of peer and self-assessment is to help close the gaps in the students' learning by making them aware of what is needed.

We shall revisit peer and self-assessment later in this book, when we discuss in more detail the role that students themselves can play in the assessment process in Chapter 8.

Metacognition

We mentioned brain-based learning approaches in Chapter 2, and it is in our considerations of formative assessment here that one aspect of these can usefully be considered, this being *metacognition*. Metacognition, put simply, involves thinking about thinking. There are obviously far more detailed and complex connotations to it than this, but for our purposes this forms a straightforward working definition. What we are discussing here in terms of assessment is the ways in which students are able to both think about, and monitor, their own learning. Developing students' skills in the process of metacognition is a necessary precondition before you and they are able to move towards peer and self-assessment. One way in which this can be introduced is suggested by Brooks:

> Students must be trained in the required metacognitive skills by teachers modelling the processes for them. Teachers can do this by sharing marking exercises with classes, using exemplification material to show how criteria are applied and how judgements are reached.

> (Brooks, 2002, p70)

Working in this way, the process of metacognition is being modelled and then operationalised in order to allow students to really think about their learning.

PRACTICAL TASK PRACTICAL TASK PRACTICAL TASK PRACTICAL TASK PRACTICAL TASK

As a plenary activity, in a class which you will be teaching soon, experiment by asking the students to spend a few minutes working in pairs and reflecting on the learning they have done during a lesson. At the end of this time, share thinking by asking the class to comment out loud on their learning; make it very clear that you are interested in this, rather than in what they have learned.

The distinction made at the end of this practical task is an important one. Students often mistakenly view learning in terms of the 'empty vessels' view we discussed in the opening chapters of this book. Here we want them to be thinking about *how* they learned, not *what*.

REFLECTIVE TASK

Think about your own learning during the course of this book. How have you learned? By reading? By applying the text to your own situation? By writing down key points? By drawing a mind-map? By reading out loud? By trying things out in the classroom? How do you know if you are a good learner? How do you know what a good learner is?

There are lots of complicated issues in this reflective task, and it is not possible to give one set of right answers which will apply to all readers of this book. This is a point that will also apply to the students in your classroom, and we know from research on learning styles that the ways in which your students learn might not be the same as you. This is why your formative assessments need to be tailored to fit the individual students with whom you are working, tailored and personalised to suit their own learning.

Distributed cognition

Making a judgement about assessment involves a complex series of mental operations, and for the students it may well be that the process of peer assessment, when carried out conjointly, allows these operations to be distributed between a number of individuals, thus distributing cognition (Salomon, 1993). The practical task above relating to the process of peer assessment involved the participants in discussion. What happens during discussion is that the very act of students talking to each other brings to the forefront some aspects of the cognitive processes involved in making assessment judgements. This makes them apparent to the students, and, helpfully, to you.

Distributing the process of assessment between a number of students can be viewed both as a good thing in its own right, and as a stage on the journey towards individual autonomy. Sharing the complex cognition involved uses dialogic discussion, and in organising this in your lessons it is important to emphasise that this is another aspect of learning where the process is at least as important as the product. Developing the capabilities of the students to discuss and reflect on their work is an important part of the learning experience. As James observes:

> *Perhaps the most crucial aspect of training students in self assessment and peer assessment is enhancing the* quality of the discourse... *Students need to be trained to ask thoughtful questions of their own work and that of their peers; they need to be helped to admit problems without risking the loss of self-esteem; they*

need to take time to puzzle over the reasons why problems have arisen; and they need to know that it is acceptable to look at a number of possible solutions before opting for a particular course of action.

(James, 1998, p177)

So we can see that these discussions concerning assessment are important, and do not simply relate to being a complex way of dealing with summative assessment, but by sharing the journey, the students will hopefully become more able to undertake the process of self-assessment by themselves. Bringing things out into the open in the form of discussions, an area to which we return later, will hopefully enable the students to become more self-aware with regard to their own learning.

Conclusion

The techniques of formative assessment we have been discussing in this chapter share the common aim of improving student learning. In an earlier chapter we investigated the notion of how in the past assessment had been 'curiously separate' from instruction. In this chapter it should be apparent that all of the aspects of formative assessment with which we have been dealing are intrinsic to the process of teaching; they are not optional bolt-on accessories. As you teach you will be making judgements all the time, and many of these judgements will be formative assessments. They will not involve giving grades, marks or levels to pieces of work, but are instead focused on taking learning forwards. This is an important concept. Formative assessment can improve learning, not by giving a gradual series of improving grades or levels, but by sharing the learning journey with students as agents in their own development. As a beginning teacher this may seem like a complex and potentially overwhelming requirement of you, but you can see how it is in the learners' best interests to do this. In subsequent chapters we shall introduce you to ideas and give you practical strategies for you to use in the classroom, which will help ease your way somewhat into this vital area.

Formative assessment is a tremendously powerful tool in the teacher's toolkit, and one of the key messages of this book is that the appropriate use of formative assessment can make substantial differences to student learning.

A SUMMARY OF **KEY POINTS**

In this chapter we have looked at four main areas of formative assessment:
> **questioning;**
> **feedback;**
> **sharing criteria;**
> **peer and self-assessment.**

We have discussed each of these in turn, and have discussed how they can be used and applied in your classroom. We have also looked at the following issues.

> **Wait time – giving students time to think before answering.**
> **Bloom's taxonomy – categorising questions.**
> **Question stems – for you to develop your own repertoire.**
> **Feedback and feedforward – helping students improve their work.**

> **Formative feedback instead of grading** – its role in shifting student perceptions.
> **Learning outcomes and assessment criteria** – forming a clear linkage between these.
> **Peer and self-assessment** – their role in helping students be responsible for their own learning.

REFERENCES REFERENCES **REFERENCES** REFERENCES **REFERENCES** REFERENCES

Assessment Reform Group (2002) Assessment for learning: 10 Principles. Cambridge: ARG.

Black, P. and Wiliam, D. (1998a) Assessment and classroom learning. *Assessment in Education,* 5(1): 68.

Black, P. and Wiliam, D. (1998b) *Inside the black box: raising standards through classroom assessment*. London: School of Education, King's College.

Bloom, B.S. (1956) *Taxonomy of educational objectives, Handbook I: The cognitive domain.* New York: David McKay Co, Inc.

Brooks, V. (2002) *Assessment in secondary schools: the new teacher's guide to monitoring, assessment, recording, reporting and accountability*. Buckingham: Open University Press.

James, M. (1998) *Using assessment for school improvement*. Oxford: Heinemann Educational.

Rowe, M.B. (1974) Wait-time and rewards as instructional variables. *Journal of Research in Science Teaching,* 11; 81–94.

Sadler, D. (1989) Formative assessment and the design of instructional systems. *Instructional Science,* 18, 119–44.

Salomon, G. (ed) (1993) *Distributed cognitions*. Cambridge: Cambridge University Press.

Torrance, H. and Pryor, J. (1998) *Investigating formative assessment*. Buckingham: Open University Press.

FURTHER READING FURTHER READING **FURTHER READING** FURTHER READING

Black, P., Harrison, C., Lee, C., Marshall, B. and Wiliam, D. (2003) *Assessment for learning: putting it into practice*. Maidenhead: Open University Press/McGraw Hill Education.

Brooks, V. (2004) Using assessment for formative purposes, in Brooks, V., Abbott, I. and Bills, L. (eds) *Preparing to teach in secondary schools*. Buckingham: Open University Press.

Clarke, S. (2005) *Formative assessment in the secondary classroom*. London: Hodder Murray.

Haydn, I. (2005) Assessment for learning, in Capel, S., Leask, M. and Turner, T. (eds) *Learning to teach in the secondary school*. London: RoutledgeFalmer.

5
Developing assessment strategies

Chapter objectives

By the end of this chapter you should have:

- **learned about integrating planning for assessment into your lessons;**
- **thought about linking learning outcomes with assessment;**
- **thought about the role of differentiation;**
- **considered the notion of academic performance being evidenced in achievement;**
- **thought about the importance of teacher judgements;**
- **considered the vital role of assessment in progression;**
- **reflected on the formative use of summative assessment.**

Professional Standards for QTS

This chapter will help you to meet the following Professional Standards for QTS:
Q7a, Q8, Q10, Q19, Q22, Q25a-d, Q26a-b, Q27, Q28, Q29

Introduction

Having considered the ways in which assessment can be used in the classroom, what we need to do now is to think about how you, as a trainee teacher, can plan for assessment to take place in your lessons. What this will entail, in fact, is for you to plan for *learning* to take place in your lessons. In earlier chapters, we have discussed how assessment should be integral to a view of teaching and learning, and we spoke briefly about a model of teaching and learning which contained and encompassed the notion of assessment within it. For the sake of convenience, a graphical representation of this model, which was shown originally as Figure 1.3, is reproduced here.

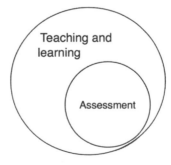

Figure 5.1 Assessment within teaching and learning

What Figure 5.1 shows is that planning for assessment is indivisible from planning for teaching and learning, and that all these elements should be considered at the same time when thinking about lessons. What this means for you is that writing lesson plans involves thinking about all of these elements as one joined-up singularity. What we are going to do now is to build on the initial work from earlier chapters and take this further. The objective for this is to help you to develop ways in which you can plan your lessons so that assessment is indeed integral to teaching and learning.

Integrating learning with assessment

There are essentially three types of planning that you are likely to be involved in at this stage of your development as a beginning teacher.

- **Long-term planning:** For a whole year group, for example, this would be an overview of the units of work that make up the learning over an academic year for a specific year cohort.
- **Medium-term planning:** For units of work; these can be on a given topic, a thematic approach, a section of an exam specification, or a sequence of learning activities.
- **Individual lesson plans:** These are fundamental to the daily work of the teacher, and involve planning for learning to take place for all students in the class, to be sequential in nature, developmental by design, and to represent the distillation of medium- and long-term planning into a specific, achievable and time-delimited activity. As Standard Q22 states, you should be able to:
  - 'Plan for progression across the age and ability range for which they are trained, designing effective learning sequences within lessons and across series of lessons and demonstrating secure subject/curriculum knowledge.'

Figure 5.2 is a graphical representation of the planning process, exemplified specifically in this instance for a Year 7 cohort. Notice how planning should be top-down, rather than bottom-up, i.e. lesson plans should flow from the overall view of learning outcomes.

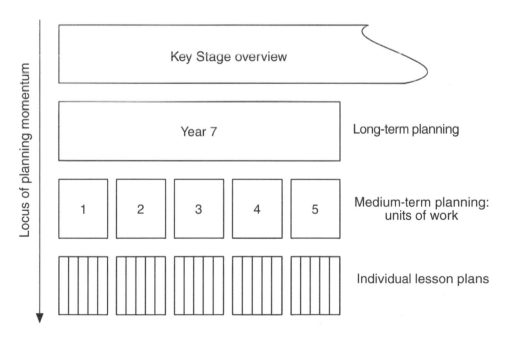

Figure 5.2 Planning sequence overview

Notice that Figure 5.2 also includes a *key stage overview* which is likely to be in the purview of the head of department, and into which you will be required to fit your medium-term and individual lesson plans. As a beginning teacher it is likely that you will need to fit in with extant plans for the key stages you will be teaching. It is also likely that in many cases you will be assigned specific units of work, which have already been written, and into which you will need to fit your individual lesson plans. For these reasons we are going to concentrate our attention on planning for and within individual lessons, in other words at the end stage of the *locus of planning momentum*. However, the general principles we shall be outlining of thinking about learning and building assessment into this planning also hold true when considering the broader aspects of medium- and longer-term planning. As these are likely to be issues you will meet later in your teaching career, our concern will remain focused on your day-to-day planning for learning.

Planning documentation

Lesson planning documentation is often specific to a course, training programme, school or college, so a common format cannot be assumed. What many lesson planning pro-formas do adopt is something of this nature.

- **Aims:** What the intentions of the lesson are, but grounded firmly in reality. Aims need to be specific to the lesson rather than generalised good intentions. They should be challenging for students in order to build on previous learning. It is often helpful if aims can be cross-referenced to the National Curriculum or exam specifications as they will be delivered in the lesson. Aims need to be specific and achievable.
- **Learning outcomes:** Learning outcomes should state clearly what the students will have learned by the end of the lesson. They should be focused on learning, rather than on the tasks that the students will complete. Key Stage 3 learning outcomes are likely to cross-reference to the National Curriculum; Key Stage 4 will cross-reference to National Curriculum and/or exam specifications; Key Stages 5/16+ will cross-refer to exam specifications. Remember that the context of the learning should be the same for all students, although activities will be differentiated to meet students' individual needs. Learning outcomes should be specific, measurable and achievable within the timeframe of the lesson.
- **Lesson body:** Often divided into three sections: starter – development – plenary. This describes what will be done during the lesson. Key activities, questions and learning sequences should be described here. Starter activities and plenary sessions need to be planned, and should have a linear progression from one to the next.
- **Assessment for learning:** This will describe how effectively the students will have met the learning outcomes. This section needs to be more than mere description. What is important here for you, the teacher, is how do you know? In other words what evidence do you have to say how you are able to judge whether (or not) the learning outcomes have been met, and to what extent?
- **Evaluation:** This is your opportunity to develop as a reflective practitioner. This section is important to your future development, and is discussed in more detail in the final chapter. However, it is important to note at this stage that comments in this section should be focused on learning, and that descriptions of student enjoyment and behaviour are only significant in terms of how they affect achievement and progress.

From this planning sequence, our concern in this chapter is for the integration of learning outcomes with assessment for learning, and how this affects and effects the activities done in the lesson body. We begin from the point of departure in Chapter 4, and take up our discussion of planning for learning.

From learning outcomes to assessment criteria

Figure 4.4 ('Formative assessment planning') in Chapter 4 took you through a number of stages of thinking about aspects of planning. In Figure 5.3 the upper part of this diagram has been extracted and collapsed somewhat.

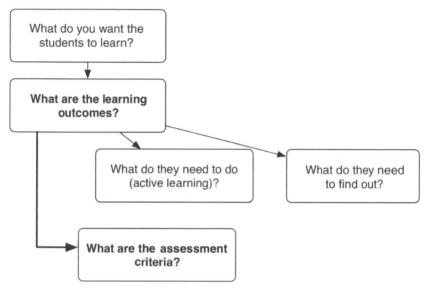

Figure 5.3 Learning outcomes and assessment criteria

In our original discussions we noted how good learning outcomes can be reapplied as assessment criteria. For many trainee teachers, and indeed for many practising teachers, we discussed how writing good learning outcomes can be problematic. We have also noted already that a common mistake made by beginning teachers is to confuse *doing* with *learning*. It is much easier to write task outcomes than it is to write learning outcomes. In a true learning outcome it is the learning which is the focus of your attention, whereas a task outcome is concerned more with action and activity, or simply with keeping the students busy.

PRACTICAL TASK PRACTICAL TASK PRACTICAL TASK PRACTICAL TASK **PRACTICAL TASK**

When you next observe teachers writing learning outcomes or lesson objectives on the board, ask yourself whether these truly are learning outcomes or whether they are task outcomes.

We discussed in Chapter 4 how you will sometimes hear teachers talking about 'good' activities to do with the students. You will also be able to find publications which are little more than collections of activities designed to occupy classes. You might think to yourself that something you have seen or experienced would make a good lesson. As we noted in our original discussions, what you need to do in these circumstances is to take a step backwards and ask yourself the question, 'What is it that the students will be learning in this?' If the answer is little or nothing, you need to consider why this activity should be done at all.

The role of differentiation

Another point we discussed with relation to formative assessment back in Chapter 4, was that of dividing up learning outcomes to allow for differentiation. There we outlined how a division into all–most–some outcomes in planning is a sensible way to begin this process. What assessment for learning should do is enable you and the students to know whether these distinctions have been met, and, if so, to what degree. In order to study this further, let us investigate some examples drawn from different curriculum areas as exemplar materials. It is important to note that although we are using specific subject areas and year groups to do this, the general principles concerned with lesson planning should be applicable across a range of ages, phases, and ability groups.

TEACHING EXAMPLE
Food technology
During Key Stage 3 students use a wide range of materials to design and make products. In this example the teacher is trying to ensure that knowledge and understanding are applied when making their product. Let us take the case of a Year 7 class preparing a salad.

The aims of this lesson are:
1. To consider aesthetics and other issues that influence their planning (1e[1]).
2. Select and use tools, equipment and processes to shape and form materials safely and accurately and finish them appropriately (2a).

The learning outcomes are:
By the end of the lesson...
...all students will have learned:
- to prepare and combine ingredients to make a salad that meets the design brief (1e, 4c, 7b);
- that a variety of ingredients can be used to prepare a salad that meets the design brief (1e, 4c, 7b);
- that ingredients can be prepared using different tools and methods of preparation (4c, 7b).

...most students will have learned:
- to prepare and combine ingredients to make a salad that meets the design brief and be able to state how the design brief has been met (1e, 4c, 7b);
- that a variety of ingredients can be used to prepare a salad that meets the design brief, and be able to suggest alternative ingredients to those that have been allocated (1e, 4c, 7b);
- that ingredients can be prepared using different tools and methods of preparation and be able to justify the choices they have made (4c, 7b).

...some students might have learned:
- to prepare and combine ingredients to make a salad that meets the design brief and be able to state how the design brief has been met, covering all points (1e, 4c, 7b);
- that a variety of ingredients can be used to prepare a salad that meets the design brief, be able to suggest alternative ingredients to those they have been allocated and indicate where the alternatives fit onto the balanced plate (1e, 4c, 7b);
- that ingredients can be prepared using different tools and methods of preparation, be able to justify the choices they have made and suggest alternative methods of preparation (4c, 7b).

---

[1] In this and subsequent examples the numbers and letters in brackets refer to the National Curriculum for the subject in question.

Notice how the learning outcomes are sequential between the all–most–some divisions. In other words, the first learning outcome for all students becomes superseded by the first learning outcome for most students, and so on. These learning outcomes can clearly be seen to contain within them the seeds for assessment for learning to take place. It will be a straightforward matter for the teacher to decide which students have achieved what aspects of the learning required from them. Notice too that some aspects of learning can only be uncovered by undertaking discussions with the students. The learning is not solely contained in the work of the individual students in terms of the final plated outcome, important aspects of the learning are involved in the processes by which these outcomes were reached.

Let us dig a little deeper into these distinctions between learning and doing. There are times when learning may be contained *in* doing, and that physical activity supported by conceptual understanding is the aim of the lesson. In this case what you will need to do is formulate learning outcomes based on the fact that the students will be *learning to do*. As an example let us consider the case of a music lesson, where the students are learning how to play a 12-bar blues.

TEACHING EXAMPLE
Music
Learning outcomes (Performing):
By the end of the lesson...
...all students:
- will have developed their understanding of chords and chord sequences by performing the chords (in root position or simple inversions) to a 12-bar blues.

...most students:
- will have developed their understanding by learning to play the 12-bar blues chords with stylistically appropriate rhythmic development.

...some students:
- will have further developed their understanding by learning to maintain the chord sequence while playing a stylistically appropriate bass-line, riff or improvisation.

This lesson involves learning to do something, in this case perform, but simply saying that 'All students will perform a 12-bar blues chord sequence' does not adequately identify the learning. This is an example of lesson which can be undertaken at a number of different levels of complexity – remember the spiral curriculum from Chapter 2. So, as this lesson could be taught from Key Stage 2 through to postgraduate level, the learning outcomes need to indicate how previously learned skills and knowledge will be developed, and that is why they are so specific. This might seem pedantic, but remember that by spending time crafting good learning outcomes, you will be making the assessment process transparent. In the case of this music lesson, the teacher will be able to know which students have achieved which learning outcome by observing the students practising, and listening to the final performances which result during the plenary stage of the lesson.

What is happening in the music lesson is that understanding is evidenced in achievement. It is clear to see that this is another way of looking at learning similar to the javelin-throwing example from earlier chapters. But what does this mean, 'understanding evidenced in achievement'? If someone tells you they can tap-dance, the proof is that they can. There are many complicated steps and routines involved in tap-dancing, and the learner needs to develop an understanding of these, but the real proof will be in practical achievement. This is a case where *knowing how* is the form of knowledge which the lesson is addressing. What the music teacher has done in the example above is to clearly state which aspects of learning are important in that particular lesson. It is quite likely that this lesson will form one of a sequence based on the 12-bar blues, and although the students may well be playing the same piece of music next lesson, the learning is likely to be different, and will arise from the teacher's evaluation and formative assessments made during the course of this lesson. In other words, the *doing* might remain similar, but it is the *learning* which alters.

The notion of understanding evidenced in achievement is patently not unique to music. Here is an example drawn from a Key Stage 4 drama lesson.

TEACHING EXAMPLE
Drama
The aim of this lesson is developing character from text. The learning outcomes are divided into two areas, creating and performing.

Creating
By the end of the lesson...
...all students will have learned
- that contextual details from the text can form a basis for creating a character.

...most students will have learned
- that contextual details from the text can suggest attitudinal features and can include these in their own created character.

...some students may have learned
- that attitudinal features drawn from the text will affect their created character's relationships and interactions with other characters.

Performing
By the end of the lesson...
...all students
- will have developed their understanding of the character in the text by including this understanding in their physical and vocal presentation of their own character.

...most students
- will have developed their understanding of the character in the text by using a range of physical and vocal means to convey their attitude.

...some students
- may have further developed their understanding of the textual character by showing, both physically and vocally, the way in which attitude has affected relationships with other characters.

Here again we can clearly see how the teacher will be able to progress from the learning outcomes to an assessment of individual students' understanding as evidenced in achievement. A less thoughtful drama teacher might have produced a simpler version, along the lines of 'all students will create a character from the text'; although this satisfies the immediacy of a lesson, notice how it misses out the complexities of the learning experience, tells the students only what they will do, and ignores the quality or level of their learning; it is a task outcome, not a learning one. We discussed in Chapter 3 how important it was to share learning outcomes with students, and in this case using the full version of the learning outcomes will enable students to become attentive and responsible for their own learning. What this will also do is to enable peer and self-assessment to take place more readily, as the students will have a clearer view of what their own learning entails, how it fits in with the learning of their peers, and, importantly, what a successful learning outcome will look like. We will explore this further in Chapter 8.

Learning evidenced in achievement need not be confined to academic or practical outcomes alone. In a Key Stage 3 art lesson on the topic of cutting a lino block, health and safety matters form an important component alongside the subject-specific learning that the teacher wants. In this next example, notice how the teacher skilfully develops these health and safety issues as part of her all–most–some learning outcomes.

TEACHING EXAMPLE
Art and design
The aims of the lesson are:
To provide opportunities for students to:
- learn and experience the principles of cutting a lino block (2b, 2c, 5c);
- base lino cutting on the relief printmaking of the German Expressionist School (4c, 5d);
- understand the safety principles of lino cutting and exercise care with the use of tools (health and safety).

The learning outcomes are:
By the end of the lesson. . .
. . . all students will have learned:
- how to cut and gain experience of, cutting a lino block using appropriate tools (2b, 2c, 5c);
- to use lino cutting tools with safety.

. . . most students will have learned:
- the skilled application of mark-making achieved with the selection of appropriate tools, showing understanding of the media (2b, 2c, 5c);
- to achieve careful and skilful manipulation of lino cutting tools.

. . . some students might have learned:
- to apply appropriate tools to achieve skilled marks in lino cutting with an expressive outcome within the style of their studied artist (4c, 5d);
- a clear understanding demonstrated in their working practice of health and safety issues.

Health and safety are not issues you can leave to chance, and this lesson shows how learning outcomes can be written to encompass this hand-in-hand with achievement.

Notice how the learning outcomes in all of these examples so far employ the sequential delineation we spoke of earlier. Sometimes, however, you may want to take a cumulative approach to differentiated learning outcomes, and ensure that all students are familiar with knowledge, skills and concepts required before you are able to move *most* or *some* students on to develop other aspects of learning. This is the approach adopted in this lesson plan by a maths teacher.

TEACHING EXAMPLE
Maths
The aims of the lesson are:
To provide opportunities for students to:
- use standard form display;
- know how to enter numbers in standard index form;
- convert between ordinary and standard index form representations.

The learning outcomes for this lesson are:
By the end of the lesson...
...all students will have learned:
- to write numbers in standard form;
- to convert numbers in standard form to ordinary numbers using a calculator;
- to make some simple calculations using standard form without a calculator.

...most students will have learned:
- to use a calculator to calculate using standard form.

...some students will have learned:
- to use standard form to make approximations and estimates.

This notion of taking a cumulative approach to learning outcomes provides a different, but still linear, route towards assessment. In the case of the maths lesson the teacher will need to differentiate by learning procedure in order to facilitate and progress student learning. This will involve the teacher in making a series of formative assessments with regard to the attainment and understanding of individual students.

Making judgements

What we have said so far in this section is that by writing clear learning outcomes you will be able to use these as assessment criteria. But what does this mean in practice, and how will you carry this out? To examine this in a little more detail let us return to the example from the food technology lesson above. The 'base level' learning outcome, the one which all students will be expected to achieve was:

- **All: that a variety of ingredients can be used to prepare a salad that meets the design brief.**

This offers an opportunity for formative assessment in that the teacher will make a judgement concerning the way the students understand this task. We know, even if we are not food technology teachers, that the notion of a salad is a specific form of dish, and we are able to formulate a hypothesis as to the sorts of ingredients that we might reasonably expect to find contained in one. In order for the teacher to be reasonably certain that all the students in the class have grasped the concept of 'salad-ness' then what she will have done is to have made a formative assessment that this is the case. This formative assessment need not be documented, it need not be a complex multi-part decision-making process, it is simply a judgement-call made by the teacher, that she can move a number of students, *most*, in the terminologies we are employing, onto the next stage in their learning. This is an important point for you to realise. Formative assessments of this nature are not big high-stakes ones, they are small, everyday decisions which you, the teacher, will make many times each lesson. The evidence required – remember we discussed having an evidence base upon which to make decisions – is that the students have evidenced their understandings either in achievement, or in discussion with you, and that as a result of these you can be reasonably confident that you can move on. There can be few things more disheartening to learners than being held back by the teacher.

From this formative assessment, that most of the students are ready to move on to the next level of learning outcome, the teacher will then move on to address the next level of learning outcome:

- **Most: that a variety of ingredients can be used to prepare a salad that meets the design brief, and be able to suggest alternative ingredients to those that have been allocated.**

Again, if you are a non-specialist food technology teacher you can still follow the logic of this learning outcome. Here the essential feature is that student achievement is evidenced in discussion. To be able to suggest alternatives does not mean they have to have the ingredients to hand. Neither does it close down learning, in that an element of creative or divergent thinking is appropriate here. The formative assessments made now will again be based on a judgement-call concerning student learning, and the final tier of learning outcome:

- **Some: that a variety of ingredients can be used to prepare a salad that meets the design brief, be able to suggest alternative ingredients to those they have been allocated and indicate where the alternatives fit onto the balanced plate.**

can now be considered, and again, this will be *evidenced* in discussion.

Progression

Notice that we have discussed the teacher considering moving students on in their learning. This does not necessarily mean that she is teaching any differently, and the same lesson body is likely to have been undertaken by all of the students. The formative assessments made with regard to learning outcomes have been done in conversation with the students as the teacher moves around the class, discussing the work done with the students, and considering the evidence from achievement and discussion. This progression in learning evidences not only differentiation by outcome, but differentiation by understanding, and the evidence is to be found in the formative assessment discussions made by the teacher as she works with her students. We shall revisit planning later in this book, particularly when we discuss using assessment data in the following chapter.

Planning for conversations

We have seen how the evidence for the judgement-calls made by the teacher arise from conversations had while teaching. These conversations are an integral part of the assessment process, and just because they are not written down does not make them any the less important. There is an overt and understandable drive in schools to raise standards via the use of assessment, but this does not mean that the only assessments that count are those which are documented or formalised. The role of informal assessment is vital in the way student learning can be developed. It relies on you and the students valuing the things you say, and being prepared to act upon each other's comments. This does not mean that you need to undervalue documented, formalised assessment procedures, but that you need to afford equal importance to the formative assessment judgements that you make, and one way you can do this is to plan for assessment-focused conversations to take place in your classroom.

The 'chalk and talk' style of teaching allows for little by way of interaction with the students. Nowadays a more interactive style of teaching is the norm, and this requires more by way of a two-way dialogue between teacher and students, and so planning for assessment-based conversations is a logical part of your development. You are likely to observe your mentors having unscripted conversations with students; this is a stage you will reach soon enough. To begin with, depending on your improvisation skills, you may find it helpful to plan the first few conversational turns you will have with your classes. You will have to 'improvise' conversations, and this involves being able to think on your feet. Chapter 3 included a list of potential stems for developing questions based on Bloom's taxonomy (Bloom, 1956). In planning for formative assessment conversations stems similar to these are likely to be useful here too.

Formative assessment conversation starting points

Having written your carefully constructed learning outcomes, what you will want to know is the way these will be evidenced in your classroom. Table 5.1 shows a number of these.

Table 5.1 Understanding evidenced...

Type of understanding	Evidenced by...	Example
Understanding evidenced in achievement	Being able to do something	Can tap-dance
Understanding evidenced in process	Being able to undertake a task, demonstrate a skill or concept, show that the student knows how to do something, even if they cannot yet evidence achievement	Knows how to do mathematical proof by induction, but has come up with the wrong answer
Understanding evidenced in product	The emergent product shows the student knows what they are doing, and this is clearly to be seen in the finished item	Has made a salad
Understanding evidenced through discussion	Knowing that, and being able to talk about it coherently	Knows that Harold lost the Battle of Hastings in 1066, and can give an account of the events leading up to this
Understanding evidenced some other way	Subject-specific ways of knowing that do not fall easily into any of the above categories	You will know these from your own specialism

The different types of understanding which you will be dealing with will require a different assessment conversation. Some are straightforward: 'Can you tap-dance, show me...'. Some less so: 'You appear to know what you should be doing, but you keep coming up with the wrong answer at the end.'

ЯЕFLECTIVE TASK
REFLECTIVE TASK

Think of a topic you will be teaching soon. Ask yourself these questions:
In what ways will understanding be evidenced?
How will I be able to access this evidence?
Do I need to ask questions to do this?
If so, what are they?
What will I do when I know that understanding has been achieved?

Your answers will obviously depend on the type and nature of your subject, and the views of knowledge (from Chapters 1 and 2) that will be involved. The different types of understanding will require you to think carefully about what will be going on in your lesson, and, importantly, how you can gain access to knowing the understandings of your students. We said earlier that these conversations are like improvisations – you need to have a clear view of the direction the dialogue should be heading in, but you need to be reactive too, and listen to, and take heed of, what the students are telling you.

The object of the last reflective task was to get you to think about understandings in your classroom. Having done this, the next stage is to plan your assessment conversations accordingly. These will clearly vary widely depending on many factors, and it is to be hoped that we have covered the ground adequately for you to do this. Sometimes trainee teachers feel that they are planning for all eventualities – you are! But in time this planning will become almost second nature, although, as we said in the case of learning outcomes, this does not mean it gets easier. Doing the planning, and making it visible in well-structured lesson plans helps you, and your tutors and mentors, to understand what you are doing. They are making formative assessments too, remember, in this case about you, and you need to evidence your understanding in achievement in the classroom. Remember that planning for assessment is the first step towards carrying it out.

The formative use of summative assessment

So far in this chapter we have been concerned mostly with formative assessment being used in order to look forward to developing learning, and have suggested ways in which you can adopt this in your classroom. It is useful at this juncture to consider that summative assessment can also be used in a formative fashion, and there are logical reasons for doing this which will also help students take their learning forwards.

We discussed marking and grading in Chapter 3. Your placement school will have a marking policy. This should give you the information you need as to how whole-school issues concerning marking and grading have been organised, and your subject mentor will be able to tell you about departmental expectations. Whatever the system is in use for you, using summative assessment in a formative fashion means building on results from tests, tasks, achievements and assignments to effect future learning. What this means in practice is that this information is useful in two ways, to you, and to the students. Figure 5.4 redraws Figure 3.1 from Chapter 3, and adds a new layer to it.

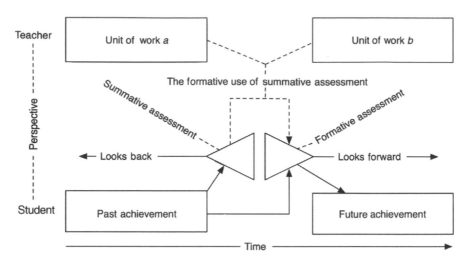

Figure 5.4 Assessment modalities revisited

What is added in Figure 5.4 are the different perspectival viewpoints of the teacher and the student. In order for summative assessment to be used effectively, the teacher needs to have a view of future work, both in terms of the future achievement of the student, and with regard to forthcoming units of work. For the sake of clarity, Figure 5.4 shows discrete units of work, but it could equally be within an existing one as a subdivision. Using summative assessment in a formative fashion means being prepared to change future teaching as a result of what is found out. This is unlikely to mean change on a large basis, but is more to do with tailoring the teaching to the needs of the classes, and tweaking emphasis. Using assessment information in this way is to be reactive to the needs of your students, not simply steamrollering on. We often hear about the demands placed on youngsters in schools; being prepared to alter your materials to better suit the learners in front of you is one way of addressing this issue.

Another aspect involved in the formative use of summative assessment is that of having discussions with students in order to interpret what marks and grades mean for them. We have already seen how grades alone can be a disincentive to students. In order to challenge this attitude you need to explain in specific terms what the individual student needs to do in order to improve next time. This should be tailored and targeted feedback, so the student has a clear idea what that means for them as an individual. Whole-class feedback, although possibly helpful in some instances, will be of little import to a student who has achieved a significantly lower grade than the rest of the group. Here you do need to focus on the individual. Remember that every behind every statistic is a real student with feelings.

So summative assessment used in a formative fashion can help take learning forward, but it needs planning for, and it requires a degree of flexibility on your part.

Conclusion

We have discussed the importance of planning for assessment, and of integrating formative assessment within your teaching. We have discussed how the things you say and the discussions you have with your students are valuable, and, linking this with the work on recording assessments which you undertook in earlier sections, should place you in a strong position to begin to think carefully about how your planning for assessment is, in fact, planning for learning. We have discussed how writing good learning outcomes is a key activity for you, and we have thought about how planning for formative assessment conversations is helpful to you in this early stage of your career.

A SUMMARY OF **KEY POINTS**

In this chapter you have:

> **learned about the importance of planning for assessment to be an integral part of teaching and learning;**

> **realised that planning for learning involves differentiation;**

> **reflected on planning documentation that you need to complete;**

> **realised how important the day-to-day judgements you make in the classroom are to developing learning;**

> **learned to appreciate the importance of assessment-based conversations.**

REFERENCES REFERENCES **REFERENCES** REFERENCES **REFERENCES** REFERENCES

Bloom, B.S. (1956) *Taxonomy of educational objectives, Handbook I: The cognitive domain.* New York: David McKay Co, Inc.

FURTHER READING FURTHER READING **FURTHER READING** FURTHER READING

Black, P., Harrison, C., Lee, C., Marshall, B. and Wiliam, D. (2003) *Assessment for learning: putting it into practice.* Maidenhead: Open University Press/McGraw-Hill Education.

Brooks, V. (2002) *Assessment in secondary schools: the new teacher's guide to monitoring, assessment, recording, reporting and accountability.* Buckingham: Open University Press.

Brooks, V. (2004) Using assessment for formative purposes, in Brooks, V., Abbott, I. and Bills, L. (eds), *Preparing to teach in secondary schools.* Buckingham: Open University Press.

Gardner, J. (2006) *Assessment and learning.* London: SAGE.

6
Assessment data

Chapter objectives

By the end of this chapter you should have:

- **thought about the differences between tangible and intangible assessment data;**
- **considered the wide range of assessment data available to you as a teacher;**
- **thought about the role of baseline assessment;**
- **reflected on how you can use data to plan for learning;**
- **reflected on the issue of ability, and what it means;**
- **thought about the notion of 'value added';**
- **thought about the National Curriculum and the use of levels to monitor and assess progress.**

Professional Standards for QTS

This chapter will help you to meet the following Professional Standards for QTS: Q1, Q3, Q13, Q19, Q26a-b, Q28

Introduction

You will have realised by this stage that assessment is a complex process, involving inter-action between teacher and student, and, when undertaken properly, it is designed with the purpose of taking learning forwards. In this chapter we are going to describe and discuss assessment data. In its simplest form, this can be thought of as existing as two ends of a continuum, *tangible* and *intangible*. Tangible data are those which exist as 'hard copy', such as the results from National Tests, GCSE results and other test scores. Intangible data are those which do not exist as such, but arise from assessment for learning dialogues, from watching students in the classroom, and from teachers making professional judgements concerning the progress of their students. The term 'data' is one which carries some consid-erable baggage, often involving quantitative numerical or statistical information. This is indeed the case for a number of the very important and useful sources of assessment data which we will be looking at during the course of this chapter, but it is also important to remember that assessment data of the intangible variety are also worthwhile, and in the case of assessment for learning, can play a part not only in developing the learning of the students in your classroom, but ultimately in terms of their tangible assessment outcomes too.

Figure 6.1 depicts a range of assessment data available to you as a teacher. It also suggests that whatever form assessment data take, the important question for you is 'what to do with these data?' You can have the most reliable and valid data possible, but there is little point in them being there unless you use them in a purposeful fashion. So, let us now turn to a consideration of a range of types of assessment data available to you, and suggest ways in which they will be of use, both now and later on in your career.

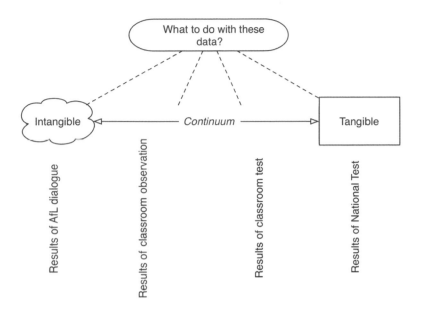

Figure 6.1 Tangible and intangible assessment data

Sources of assessment data

You are likely to encounter a number of sources of assessment data while you are in schools. These have given rise to a whole lexicon of terminologies, with associated acronyms of their own, and include the following.

- Key Stages 2 and 3 test results (National Tests).
- Other end-of-key stage (EOKS) data, such as teacher assessments (TA) and National Curriculum levels.
- Results from the National Foundation for Educational Research NfER–Nelson Cognitive Ability Tests (CATs) used by schools, often in Year 7.
- Fischer Family Trust (FFT) data.
- MidYis (University of Durham Middle Years information system) tests used during Key Stage 3.
- Yellis (University of Durham Year 11 information system) tests used during Key Stage 4.
- DfES Pupil Achievement Tracker (DfES PAT); this is a development from the previous 'Autumn Package', and School-focused Achievement and Assessment tables (formerly known as the PANDA).
- Contextual Value Added (CVA) statistics.
- 11+ examination information.
- Free School Meals (FSM) information.
- Special Educational Needs (SEN) information, including Statements and Individual Education Plans (IEPs).
- Students for whom English is an additional language (EAL).
- Ethnicity.
- Reading age.
- Baseline assessment data.
- Data generated by the school.
- Your own assessment and other data.

This list can be thought of conveniently as dividing into three areas:

- **data which are produced outside the school;**
- **data from inside the school;**
- **your own personal data.**

Each of these performs a different function, and the impact that they have on you at this stage in your career will vary in a number of ways.

Commercial data packages

In order to know if students in secondary schools are improving, it is important to know what their starting position is. For this reason many schools look at baseline assessment data, either produced by teachers themselves, building on Key Stages 2 and 3 National Tests and TA assessment data, including end-of-key stage information and National Curriculum levels, or by using a commercial package designed for this purpose, such as MidYis and Yellis (CEM website), Fischer Family Trust data (FFT website), or the NfER–Nelson CAT test (NFER–Nelson website). What many of these packages do is to try to predict students' future achievements based on statistical analysis of a number of factors. This information is used by schools to set targets for individual student achievements, and to monitor how students are doing as they progress through school. It will be useful for you to find out which of these packages your school uses, and to look at some of the data they produce for classes you teach. It is likely that your school will have a person in charge of assessment who will be able to talk to you about how the school uses this information, and what you might be able to use it for.

Using data to set targets is a complex analytical procedure, and the Fischer Family Trust recommends that teachers also use their professional judgement in these situations:

> *Be aware that the accuracy of FFT estimates varies. They are, for the most part, based upon prior attainment in core subjects. Teachers should never use FFT estimates to lower targets set by the school. If they 'disagree' with the estimate, and think the student can do better, then they should be confident to set a higher target.*

> (FFT, 2007)

This is an important point. Many of these packages are using statistical regression analysis to calculate trends. You, on the other hand, are teaching real individual students, and need to frame your decisions accordingly.

Underachievement

What many of these packages will do, however, is to help you with early diagnosis of students who might be underachieving. CAT scores, for example, are based on a range of testing regimes, and will produce figures which should prove helpful in deciding, in consultation with more experienced teachers, whether individual students are not doing as well as they might. It will then be up to the subject department, you, and your mentors, as to what action will be appropriate in each of these cases.

Using data to plan for learning

The point made above, that you will be teaching individual students, is a key message of assessment. The data available to you have to be incorporated in your teaching in a way which is appropriate. Maybe you found the list at the beginning of this chapter a little overwhelming? Do not worry, as you spend more time in schools the ways in which statistical information can be used will become clearer. Your biggest concern will be with the students you teach on a lesson-by-lesson basis, and this is how it should be. So how can you use assessment data purposefully?

It is quite likely that in your planning for units of work and the individual lesson plans that arise from them that you will have a section entitled 'prior learning' or 'evidence of prior achievement'. It is in these sections, which are designed to provoke you into thinking about this area, that you can incorporate some of the assessment data we have discussed.

> **PRACTICAL TASK** PRACTICAL TASK PRACTICAL TASK PRACTICAL TASK PRACTICAL TASK
>
> Think about the classes you will be teaching next time you are in school. What information has the school given you about them? Find it now, and think about what it is telling you.
>
> If you have already begun teaching classes, what use did you make of this information?

The answers to this will obviously depend on the school, how much information is available, and what your mentors have decided to share with you. Let us consider an assessment issue which is common in many school settings, that of ability.

Ability

> **REFLECTIVE TASK**
> REFLECTIVE TASK
>
> When you use the term 'ability', what do you mean, exactly?

Let us consider a range of possible answers to this question. This is an area where the school will be likely to give you a range of information. Some schools are themselves constituted around the notion of ability in their students. Thus grammar schools generally have some sort of selection procedure to determine who gets into them; this is usually referred to as ability testing, often measured by the 11+ examination. Is this what you meant by ability in your answer? Maybe instead you were thinking about the ways in which students are grouped for lessons? In this case ability groupings would refer to the way in which students are grouped together within classes. The common terms for these are as follows.

- **Setting:** Where students are grouped together for ability in certain subjects areas, thus students can be in different ability groups for maths and English, for example.
- **Streaming:** Where students are grouped hierarchically into classes based upon a general notion of ability (often a conflation of mathematics and English scores).
- **Banding:** Where students are placed into one of a small number of broad ability bands for all subjects.
- **Mixed ability:** Where students are not grouped according to any notion of ability.

If you teach a subject where setting is done, how is this calculated? Is there a gender balance? If you do not teach in a subject where setting is done, how are the students grouped for your lesson? Does this matter?

In fact the very notion of ability itself is a problematic construct. As we discussed in Chapter 2, Howard Gardner, an American academic, was worried by the notion of a single figure assessment of intelligence, the intelligence quotient (IQ) score, and as a result advanced a theory that people have a range of abilities (Gardner, 1983, 1999), rather than a single fixed one.

This thinking about ability should lead you to question what is meant by the term. The whole drive towards identifying gifted and talented (G&T) students is based on the premise that ability is not equal in all areas. A student who is a talented musician may not be an able geographer, so having a single construct of 'ability' for this child may miss out some important characteristics of their personality.

Contextual value added

The packages we discussed earlier are based on the premise that prior attainment is a good guide to future performance. In addition you should have Key Stage 2 data available for your Key Stage 3 classes, Key Stage 2 and Key Stage 3 data for your Key Stage 4 classes, and Key Stages 2–4 and GCSE and other 16+ results for your post-16 students. This is a wealth of information, and it will hopefully show that the students in your school are making steady progress as they move through their education. But is that enough? One of the arguments against league tables in their 'raw' form was that they did not take account of the differing intakes that schools have. As the DfES says on its website:

> *Value added measures have been used in the Achievement and Attainment Tables (formerly known as Performance Tables) since 2002. They measure the attainment of students in comparison to students with similar prior attainment; this is fairer than using raw outcomes since schools can have very different levels of attainment on entry. But there are many other factors that are related to the progress that students make in a school, such as levels of deprivation or special educational needs. Contextual value added aims to take account of these factors when measuring the effectiveness of a school or the progress made by individual students.*

> (DfES, 2005)

Contextual value added (CVA) tables involve a series of complex calculations to show the difference a school makes to the education of its students. The objective for schools is to try to do better than a simple straight-line average improvement. Schools which do this are said to offer a better CVA than schools which do not.

Using National Curriculum levels

In an effort to try to measure how much development has taken place over time within a key stage, many schools are employing National Curriculum levels on a regular basis to measure attainment. It may well be that this is the case in your school. However, this can be a problematic methodology of which you might need to be wary. Trying to use National Curriculum levels to measure a single piece of work will mean that you will have difficulty providing a range of evidence.

A single piece of work will not cover all the expectations set out in a level description. It will probably provide partial evidence of attainment in one or two aspects of a level description. If you look at it alongside other pieces of work covering a range of contexts you will be able to make a judgement about which level best fits a student's overall performance.

(NC Science website)

(Similar statements are to be found on the National Curriculum website for a wide range of National Curriculum subjects.)

In fact, the National Curriculum website counsels against using levels in this way, and many of the subject websites carry the warning on the 'About the [*subject name*] attainment target and level descriptions' page: 'Please note, level descriptions are not designed to be used to "level" individual pieces of work' (NC English website). This does not mean that you should not use National Curriculum levels to measure progress, but that you should use them holistically, look at aspects of achievement from a range of statements, and then make a 'best fit' judgement as to which will best inform you as to what the student in question has done. Do not be surprised if you reveal achievement from a number of different National Curriculum levels; this is why the 'best fit' judgement will be required.

PRACTICAL TASK PRACTICAL TASK PRACTICAL TASK PRACTICAL TASK PRACTICAL TASK

Take a range of work from a student you have been teaching. How many different National Curriculum levels does this student's work involve? What is your 'best fit' level judgement for them? Discuss this with your mentor. Do they agree with your judgement?

Using National Curriculum levels to develop learning

A common way of employing the National Curriculum levels is for teachers to rewrite them into 'student-speak'. Indeed, you may well be encouraged to do this for yourself for different units of work which you are working on. However, remember to go back to the original level statements when you come to make a judgement, not your re-written ones.

> ### CLASSROOM STORY
> A beginning geography teacher noticed that in her school 'knowledge of volcanoes' was listed as 'level 5'. When she asked her mentor about this she found that the department had rewritten the National Curriculum levels in terms of specific knowledge outcomes. The beginning teacher wrote a reflective assignment on this, and discussed her findings at a departmental meeting. As a result the department changed their rewriting of the levels.

Remember that National Curriculum levels will show slow progress; levels 3–4 are typical at the end of Key Stage 2, and levels 5–6 are typical for the end of Key Stage 3. The difference between the end of Key Stage 2 and the end of Key Stage 3 is three years, so students are unlikely to go up a whole level over a short time span.

Using assessment data to inform planning

So, you have information from the school and external sources that tell you about the range of abilities that the students in your teaching group have; what do you now do to start thinking about teaching and learning? This is where your own data need to come into play. You have the school's information – how does this tally with your own? Does it show that some students are underperforming, or doing better than expected? An important thing to remember is the notion of challenge. You want to develop learning in your classes, not let it gently stagnate. We have discussed the problems of using National Curriculum level data to investigate achievement; what other avenues are open to you? Think back to Chapter 5 where we discussed learning outcomes, and how these could become assessment criteria. It is these learning outcomes, and the assessment criteria which derive from them, which will be important to you in your everyday use of assessment. These will form the basis of your judgements as to what to do to take learning forward for the individual students in your care.

Assessment criteria for each lesson will have been suggested in your *all–most–some* learning outcome planning. What you will need to do is decide which students come into which category, and what evidence you have for making this decision. There are two contrasting dangers for beginning teachers in planning in this way:

- **only taking account of the 'top and tail' of each class, the high achievers and the underachievers;**
- **only aiming teaching and learning to the middle of the achievement spectrum of the class.**

Each of these is problematic in its own way, and yet it is not uncommon to find beginning teachers operating both on different occasions during their school placements. With large classes you need to think about personalising learning for each of the students in the class. One way of doing this is to devise simple, straightforward ways in which you can monitor and record achievement. If you write three learning outcomes for each lesson, one each for all–most–some, and have 30 students in your class, then this would give 30 separate assessments to record each lesson. If you teach a subject where you only see the students once a week this could be time-consuming. Better to decide on key learning outcomes for a unit of work or, if it is a long unit, to subdivide it, and use these as key attainment features which you will use as the basis for your assessments. Some teachers find it helpful to use hierarchic terminology deriving from the early days of the National Curriculum:

- **working towards...**
- **working at...**
- **working beyond....**

To help simplify this many teachers have devised shorthand code ways of recording this information in their mark books, and you will find more details of this, and related matters, when we look in Chapter 9 at ways of recording assessment information. The important thing for us now is in considering how you will be able to use this, and other assessment data in order to inform planning.

We have discussed on many occasions the notion that assessment underpins all of your work in the classroom, and recording significant achievement with regard to learning outcomes is a key way you can develop evidence to help with your planning. We have also discussed formative assessment, and it is to linking the various forms of evidence, particularly assessment for learning, that we turn now.

Building lessons from assessment data

As we have observed throughout this book, the aspect of planning which is most likely going to be of significant concern to you is the day-to-day planning for lessons. In Chapter 5 we considered the way in which lesson plans come from an overview of the curriculum, and what we need to do now is consider how this can be operationalised by you.

When teaching a unit of work, it is not uncommon to have a number of classes in a year cohort following the same plan simultaneously. It is at this lesson-by-lesson planning stage that the use of assessment data should be most apparent in the way you think about the achievements of your classes. Starting from a common opening lesson, it is highly likely that by the second lesson in a unit different classes will be working at different speeds, or with differing outcomes. What this means is that although you can have a common opening lesson in a sequence, you will need to plan for differentiated learning from the second lesson onwards. Figure 6.2 builds on Figure 5.2 from Chapter 5, in that it shows a graphical representation of this planning process for three separate classes following the same unit of work.

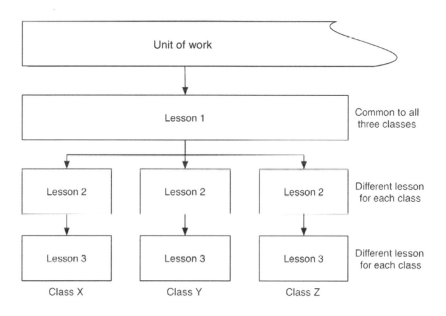

Figure 6.2 Differentiated planning

From the unit of work, you will produce a common lesson plan for the first lesson. At the end of this lesson you will evaluate what has been taking place, and how effectively your learning outcomes have been met. Using this information you will then plan for the second lesson in the sequence, and, as no two classes are alike, it is probable that your second lessons will differ from each other, possibly only in a small way. In a similar fashion the third lesson for each class will be built on assessment material, and it is possible that you will find that although you are following a common unit of work, the lessons become more widely differentiated as you and the class progress. If you think back to the locus of planning momentum we discussed in Chapter 5, the way of working we are describing here operationalises this on a daily basis in your differentiated planning for classes X, Y and Z.

The nature of the assessment data that you will be using to plan these differentiated lessons comes from both tangible and intangible sources. Your own evaluations, based on your perceptions of how the lesson went, are one source, as are formative assessment conversations you have had, dialogues with students, and your professional judgement concerning progress that has been made. It is important to recognise that the intangible assessment data can be as important to you in your planning as the tangible data from student test scores, and other summative assessment data which you have.

Quantity and quality of assessment data

Grades really cover up failure to teach. A bad instructor can go through an entire quarter leaving absolutely nothing memorable in the minds of his class, curve out the scores on an irrelevant test, and leave the impression that some have learned and some have not. But if the grades are removed the class is forced to wonder each day what it's really learning. The questions, What's being taught? What's the goal? How do the lectures and assignments accomplish the goal? become ominous. The removal of grades exposes a huge and frightening vacuum.

(Pirsig, 1974, p204)

In this quotation from Pirsig, the American education system of the 1970s is being critiqued, but there are a number of truths in it for schools in many countries today. Different subject areas generate different typologies of assessment data. The results of a maths test are different from a teacher's comments on a painting, but they are both examples of real classroom assessments. Sometimes there is a tendency for beginning teachers to be in awe of more experienced colleagues with 'weighty' mark books. This need not be the case. Collecting evidence of recordable assessment data comes more readily in some subjects than others, and modes of contact mean that some teachers teach fewer classes more frequently, again generating a different type of assessment data. Pirsig is also referring to not sharing grades with students, another topic we cover elsewhere, but let us for the moment concentrate on his notion that 'grades really cover up failure to teach'. This is contentious still today. Assessment for learning should mean that nowadays we view assessment far more widely than simply a collection of summative grades. This is a key message. We have talked in this chapter about using assessment data to plan for learning. What we have eschewed deliberately is the notion of 'one-size-fits-all lessons', where grades really would cover up a failure to plan for learning.

The quality of the assessment data you collect from your classes will obviously vary from lesson to lesson, but what is important for you is that the data carry some form of meaning. This is why you will probably be advised to write your lesson evaluations as soon after the lesson as possible, when the details are fresh in your memory. Writing evaluations might seem a chore at times, but they offer a useful source of evidence for planning for your next lesson.

Integrating different types of assessment data

We have looked at assessment data both from external sources, and those which you collect yourself. The final piece in the jigsaw is considering how these various sources of assessment data come together to give you a full picture of the progress of your students.

The personalisation of learning is a key feature of many current learning initiatives, and is an area in which we go into more detail in the next chapter. For you, having knowledge of your students plays a key part in your being able to personalise the learning experience for all the students in all your classes; after all, as the initiative says, 'every child matters'. The external data sources we discussed at the beginning of this chapter will be able to provide you with an overview as to the likely potential achievement of individual students you are teaching. However, this information is not a 'magic bullet', and it will be up to you to do something purposeful with this information. The ingredient which is needed is your knowledge of the students you teach, based on formative assessments made during the course of teaching, from summative assessments, and from marks and grades. The key element in personalising learning for the students will be you, and you need to synthesise all of the sources of data we have been discussing in order to produce differentiated learning plans for your classes. We have emphasised the importance of *all–most–some* learning outcomes, and what you will find, after you have been teaching a class for a while, is that you will have a good idea as to which students will fall into which category. Beware the self-fulfilling prophecy though – it is equally important to have high expectations for all the students that you teach.

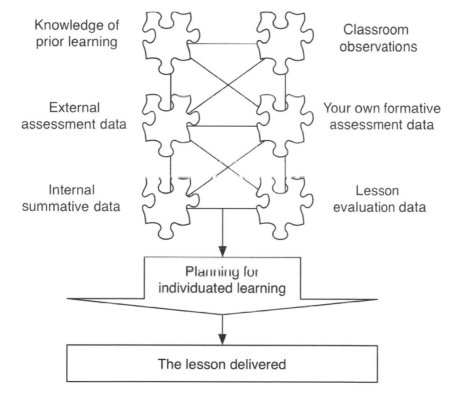

Figure 6.3 The lesson delivered

Lifting your planning off the paper

Figure 6.3 shows some of the stages which go together in the planning for a lesson. There could well be more parts of the jigsaw which you will have to assemble for your own planning to be effective. We have discussed the importance of planning at some length, but it is important that you are able to make your lessons come alive; you need to lift the planning off the paper and deliver lessons where you really do address the differentiated learning needs of all of the students in your classes.

The timeframe

Some aspects of teaching and learning happen with what seems frightening rapidity, whereas the prospect of having a view of teaching and learning over a longer time period, say a term, is one which as a beginning teacher you may feel is hard to grasp. Learning can be thought of as a cumulative process which happens over time. You are the person who has the overview, and you need to think about what progress your students will be making over a lesson, over a series of lessons, and over longer timeframes. The way you add value to learning is to ensure that you keep pushing the level of challenge for all your classes. Knowing statistically the potential of your students is one tool available to you, you need to keep thinking about maintaining the pressure on your students so that they are steadily making progress. This longer-term view of teaching will come more readily to you once you have passed the beginning teacher's natural concern with the immediacy of the classroom. However, even at this early stage of your career it is worth occasionally taking a step back from the complexity of day-to-day life in the classroom, and allowing yourself time to think about the bigger picture.

Conclusion

A common request from beginning teachers is 'tell us what to do, and we'll do it'. This assumes that mentors, lecturers and trainers somehow have a hidden book of answers which they are deliberately not sharing with you. This is far from the case. The specificities of every classroom, in every school, are unique. You need to apply the things you are being told, and use the information you are being given in order to plan and work effectively in your own situation. This chapter has dealt with many complex aspects of assessment data, but has been deliberately light on 'tips for teachers' as to how you can use them. We have warned against you delivering 'one-size-fits-all lessons' to your students, and the same thing applies here. You need to take from this chapter the information which will be pertinent to you, in your classroom, in your school. This will enable you to personalise the agenda for yourself, and then, building on this foundation, personalise learning for the students in your care. It is to the issues surrounding using assessment in the classroom that we turn in the next chapter.

A SUMMARY OF **KEY POINTS**

In this chapter we have dealt with and discussed the following issues.
> **tangible and intangible data;**
> **what to do with the data;**
> **sources of assessment data:**
   – **external**
   – **internal;**
> **using data to plan for learning;**
> **the nature of ability;**
> **using National Curriculum levels;**

> differentiated planning from assessment data;
> quantity and quality of assessment data;
> making your lesson come 'off the page';
> the importance of challenge;
> the time frame of cumulative learning;
> the personalisation agenda for you and your students.

REFERENCES REFERENCES **REFERENCES** REFERENCES **REFERENCES** REFERENCES

CEM website:

    www.cemcentre.org/RenderPage.asp?LinkID=11410000 (MidYis) (accessed June 2007)

    www.cemcentre.org/RenderPage.asp?LinkID=11510000 (Yellis) (accessed June 2007)

DfES PAT **www.standards.dfes.gov.uk/performance/**

DfES 2005: Standards website: **www.standards.dfes.gov.uk/performance/1316367/CVAinPAT2005/** (accessed June 2007)

FFT website:

    www.fischertrust.org/ (accessed June 2007)

FFT 2007: Making best use of FFT estimates. Available online at: **http://www.fischertrust.org/getdownload.aspx?96** (Accessed June, 2007)

Gardner, H. (1983) *Frames of Mind*, London: Heinemann.

Gardner, H. (1999) *Intelligence reframed*. New York: Basic Books.

NC English Website **www.ncaction.org.uk/subjects/english/targets.htm** (accessed June 2007)

NfER-Nelson website: **www.nfer-nelson.co.uk/education/resources/cat3/cat3.asp#intro** (accessed June 2007)

Pirsig, R. (1974) *Zen and the art of motorcycle maintenance*. London: Vintage.

FURTHER READING FURTHER READING **FURTHER READING** FURTHER READING

Black, P., Harrison, C., Lee, C., Marshall, B. and Wiliam, D. (2003) *Assessment for learning: putting it into practice*. Maidenhead: Open University Press/McGraw-Hill Education.

Brooks, V. (2002) *Assessment in secondary schools: the new teacher's guide to monitoring, assessment, recording, reporting and accountability*. Buckingham: Open University Press.

Hedger, K. and Jesson, D. (1998) *The numbers game: using assessment data in secondary schools*. Shrewsbury: Shropshire County Council.

James, M. (1998) *Using assessment for school improvement*. Oxford: Heinemann Educational.

7
Using assessment in the classroom

Chapter objectives

By the end of this chapter you should:

- **understand the issues associated with using assessment in the classroom and how this affects processes of teaching and learning;**
- **be able to create a positive classroom atmosphere for assessment in which the physical, emotional and perceptual needs of students are supported;**
- **use a range of strategies to enhance students' motivation through intrinsic and extrinsic models;**
- **integrate strategies for assessment within your teaching in ways that will enhance your own work and maximise your students' chances of success.**

Professional Standards for QTS

This chapter will help you to meet the following Professional Standards for QTS: Q11, Q12, Q26, Q27, Q28

Introduction

This chapter is all about how you can use assessment in the classroom. As with other chapters in this book, it will have a twin function. Firstly, it is about how you can develop assessment practices that are embedded or integrated within your teaching. In other words, teaching and assessment are holistic and symbiotic. Secondly, it is about how your students' learning can be enhanced, maximised and supported through your skilful pedagogy.

So far, we have looked at a number of key concepts including summative assessment, formative assessment, principles for recording assessment and much more besides. In this chapter, and the chapters that follow, we are going to consider, in detail, how these important broad principles outwork themselves in the context of your classroom practice. We are going to develop some practical applications of these principles for you to consider and work through in your own teaching.

In this chapter, we are going to take a general look at how you use assessment in the classroom. It is going to be a practical take on the issues that you will be facing during your early attempts at teaching. In the subsequent chapters, we will be exploring in rather more depth some of the issues raised here. You could think of this chapter as being a broad overview of the main themes that you'll need to consider as you begin to develop a holistic teaching approach with assessment at its core.

During the chapter, we are going to consider the following key points.

1. How to create a positive classroom atmosphere for assessment.
2. Individual motivation for learning is at the heart of assessment in the classroom.
3. Ensuring that assessment is integrated within your teaching.

Hopefully you can sense a progression in the above key points. We are starting with the classroom itself, the physical, emotional and social environment that is created, and the importance that this plays in creating a positive atmosphere for assessment. Within this 'space', our students arrive and need to be considered and treated as individuals, with careful thought given to their individual needs and how principles of assessment apply to them and their learning. Finally, we'll be considering more general ideas and issues associated with the integration of assessment within your teaching.

Creating a positive classroom atmosphere for assessment

The general atmosphere in a classroom can have a direct impact on students' chances of learning successfully. Creating a positive learning environment in your classroom is the first step that you will need to take in the journey towards using assessment effectively. But what do we mean when we talk about the general 'atmosphere' in a classroom? For our purposes here, we are talking about the physical, emotional (or affective) and perceptual (especially students' self-efficacy) dimensions of a classroom environment. These will all impinge on the creation of a positive assessment atmosphere.

The classroom's physical environment

Firstly, the classroom's physical environment needs to be considered. The environment should promote the learning atmosphere that you want to develop. This will have an effect on a number of things, some of which are within your control and some of which you won't be able to control. But you should be aware of them all. Here is a list of some of the most common physical environmental features that will all impact on your teaching and your students' learning.

1. Seating: the quality of seating and the arrangement of seats around the room.
2. Desks: are they necessary? How should they be arranged?
3. Combination of seating and desks with larger open spaces. Have a look at a range of primary school classrooms to see how the relationship between furniture and open spaces can be maximised for learning.
4. Storage: where do students store their belongings (books, bags, other personal effects, etc.)? Are they accessible? Do they need to be?
5. The visual environment through displays of work, posters and other resources.
6. The quality of lighting in the room. How many times have you been distracted by that flickering light or the annoying hum that it generates?
7. The air quality and temperature. You might not have much control over either of these, but personal preferences for heat or fresh air may not correspond with those of your students.
8. The provision and location of other resources, including books, items of other equipment, ICT, etc. Issues of where these are positioned and how accessible they are will have an effect on their use and integration within the classroom.

In addition to these, you will have to consider the general health and safety issues associated with the classroom's physical environment and make sure that these are in line with the school's policy. In particular, you should think about the ways in which students move around your room to access desks, seating areas, resources, etc. and make sure there is nothing that impedes their movement or places them at risk.

What are the physical aspects of a classroom environment that generate an atmosphere for learning? Spend some time analysing the physical environment of a classroom that you have to teach in regularly. Identify some of the positive and negative physical environmental elements. Start with the list above, but there are probably others that you can identify too. What are the consequences of these physical arrangements on the process of teaching and learning? In particular, what effect might they have on processes of assessment?

Chapman and King (2005) have a good, practical application of these issues in their 'Yuk Spots/Bright Spots' hunt (Chapman and King 2005, pp13–18). Basically, Yuk Spots are spots that need to be improved and Bright Spots are places or spaces that 'brighten, enhance and support a positive learning environment' but that need to be maintained. Through a simple survey mechanism that you or your students could do, this simple process analyses the classroom environment for these different types of spots and establishes a plan for improvement. It is an interesting exercise. Attempting to get a student-centric view of the classroom's learning environment and its physical dimensions is certainly a worthy goal. Why not ask students which aspects of the classroom space inhibit or enhance their opportunity to learn effectively?

The classroom's influence on students' affective domain

Equally important to the construction of a good physical environment for teaching and learning is the construction of a positive affective domain that positively influences students' emotions including their mental disposition, their level of interest and their self-motivation. Perhaps this is more difficult to achieve as it goes beyond the physical dimension (although this is important) and begins to impact on what we do as teachers. This is especially the case when we focus on assessment, which students could easily perceive as something that is done to them rather than being done with them.

REFLECTIVE TASK

What are the factors that affect students' emotional or affective response to learning in the classroom? What evidence could I observe or harness to help in the identification of positive or negative emotional responses to teaching, learning and assessment in the classroom environment?

Goleman's research on emotional intelligence is an interesting framework for our consideration here (Goleman, 1998). He describes students' intellectual capacity as working 'in concert' with their emotion. You can begin to see this in evidence when you note students' emotional responses to assessment processes, whether they are formative or summative. Perhaps students become anxious or frustrated; maybe they show disappointment or embarrassment, pleasure or exhilaration. Either way, or perhaps every way, we can see that students' emotional responses to learning are important facets that need careful handling. As an example, Chapman and King (2005, p 20) take a range of Goleman's identified emotional intelligences and characterise these for assessment activity in the classroom. To these, we have added a number of questions for you to consider as you begin to think through how assessment should work in your classroom.

1. Self-awareness
- **Understands feelings.**

- **Knows strengths and needs.**
- **Possesses self-confidence.**

To what extent do your chosen assessment processes build up an individual student's self-awareness and self-confidence?

How closely can you monitor an individual student's emotional response to an assessment process and seek to understand their individual perception of it at an emotional level?

2. Self-regulation
- **Delays gratification to pursue goals.**
- **Works to complete personal and academic tasks.**
- **Possesses the ability to recover from set-backs.**

To what extent does assessment empower individual students to make their own choices about what matters or counts in a particular teaching episode?

What impact would a greater degree of self-regulation in your classroom have on the range and type of data that you need to collect for your own assessment practice and how would this relate to wider school priorities and initiatives?

3. Motivation
- **Shows initiative.**
- **Has an innate desire to improve.**
- **Keeps trying after failure.**

Are your assessment practices primarily linear or cyclical? Do they give students an opportunity to keep trying and so build on their natural desire to improve?

How does the timing of particular assessment processes build a natural sense of student motivation through a particular task or series of tasks? When considering your longer-term plans, how can you develop positive assessment strategies that will ensure that students remain committed, involved and motivated to your subject?

4 Empathy
- **Feels what others are feeling.**
- **Respects diverse views of other individuals.**
- **Is loyal and supportive.**

How can we remain sensitive and empathetic to individual students throughout the process of assessment?

In what ways can you model appropriate responses, communicate sensitively and share emotional feelings with your students in response to the outcomes of assessment processes?

5. Social skills
- **Is a vital team member.**
- **Communicates effectively through verbal and non-verbal communication.**
- **Gets along with others.**
- **Learns during individual, paired and group work.**

Have you got a range of assessment strategies in place that emphasise the importance of social skills? Do your students know that assessment is not only about their individual effort and attainment but also about their ability to work constructively with others?

Have you developed a range of teaching activities that allow for the full range of interactions between students through individual study, paired work and group work? How can whole-class teaching contain and promote these social processes and how can you assess them in a meaningful and personalised way for each student?

Perhaps you found some of these questions quite difficult. That is because many of them challenge us to go beyond a consideration of what students produce and focus on who students are. This is always going to be harder and require a greater degree of skill and understanding. It is something that we will return to below. But for now, the final point is that we should, as teachers, be modelling these behaviours for our students to see. We don't know what your view is of young people today. Many commentators believe that they lack credible role models and are fed a prepackaged diet of knowledge limited by curriculum and examination requirements. We should be a humanising influence on our students' whole personalities and model these vital attributes.

Generating a positive sense of self-efficacy in students

Finally in this section on creating a positive classroom atmosphere for assessment, we will turn briefly to the importance of generating a positive learning environment for all students. There is an increasing literature in education about the need to encourage students' self-efficacy. Self-efficacy can be defined as:

> *An impression that one is capable of performing in a certain manner or attaining certain goals. It is a belief that one has the capabilities to execute the courses of actions required to manage prospective situations. Unlike efficacy, which is the power to produce an effect (in essence, competence), self-efficacy is the belief (whether or not accurate) that one has the power to produce that effect.*
>
> (Ormrod, 2006)

There are obvious links between self-esteem and self-efficacy. At a basic level, self-esteem relates to a person's sense of self-worth, whereas self-efficacy relates to a person's perception of their ability to reach a goal. Let's take learning to play tennis as an example. If, at this moment, you are a terrible tennis player it is likely that you will have poor efficacy in regard to tennis playing. You will probably find it hard to believe that you have the capabilities or power to produce the necessary effect or competence to play tennis effectively. But this wouldn't need to affect your sense of self-esteem. Perhaps you are not that bothered about not being able to play tennis. In other words, you're not investing your self-esteem in this area. It's unrelated and not important.

Bandura (1997) points to four sources that affect self-efficacy. These are very valuable in our consideration as to how to create a positive classroom atmosphere for learning.

1. Experience
The role of a 'mastery experience' is the most important factor in deciding a person's self-efficacy. Simply put, success raises self-efficacy and failure lowers it. Bandura makes the point that children will not be easily fooled by empty praise and condescension. While

artificial bolstering of their self-esteem is often what they are offered in many learning experiences, real strength and the construction of a positive sense of identify and self-efficacy are only achieved by 'wholehearted and consistent recognition of real accomplishment, that is, achievement that has meaning in their culture'.

As teachers, it will be vital that we take every opportunity to build up our students through the use of praise and positive reinforcement. Praise for the sake of praise won't work. In fact, according to Bandura this will have a negative effect. But genuine, authentic praise and encouragement for your students' efforts, done systematically and regularly, will build up their sense of self-efficacy and make your classroom environment a healthy one in which success and achievement is valued.

2. Modelling or vicarious experience
This is a process of comparison between people. When you see someone succeeding at something, your self-efficacy will increase; and when you see someone failing, your sense of self-efficacy will decrease. Essentially, if a student can see someone else doing something successfully, the feeling that they can do it too will be enhanced. This process is more effectual when a student can see himself or herself as similar to the person providing the model. Watching Wayne Rooney score goals for Manchester United will only achieve so much! Most of us will never be able to succeed in football at that level. If a student who is perceived as having similar ability succeeds, this will be much more likely to increase an observing student's self-efficacy. Modelling is a powerful influence, especially when students are unsure of themselves.

The use of modelling or the provision of vicarious experiences has clear applications for the classroom setting. The careful involvement of students in practical tasks, demonstrations or presentations can have a very positive influence on those watching. Of course, these students need to be seen to succeed or, at least, have their efforts positively rewarded by the teacher. Remember that, if you see someone like yourself fail at a particular task, that will decrease your self-efficacy unless you have a very strong sense of self-esteem that can be isolated or divorced from the relevant experience.

3. Social persuasions
Social persuasions relate to your conversations with people, and particularly the encouragement or discouragement that these contain. These can have a strong influence on one's sense of confidence. While positive persuasion increases self-efficacy, negative persuasions decrease it. Beware! Bandura believes that it is generally easier to decrease someone's self-efficacy than it is to increase it!

This is a vital theme that will be considered further in Chapter 8. For now, your conversations with students are a crucial part of your armoury in building up a sense of achievement and providing the positive classroom environment within which educational achievement is nurtured and valued. Similarly, students will need to be taught or reminded about the power of words when giving feedback to each other in peer-assessment exercises.

4. Physiological factors
Finally, in unusual and stressful situations, most people will exhibit signs of distress such as the shakes, aches and pains, fatigue, fear, nausea, etc. A person's perceptions of these responses can markedly alter their sense of self-efficacy. Bandura gives a very relevant example for us as teachers. If you get 'butterflies in your stomach' before teaching a

lesson and you have low self-efficacy, you may take this as a sign of your own inability. The consequent effect will be a further decrease in your self-efficacy. In contrast, if you have a higher level of self-efficacy it is likely that you will interpret such physiological signs as normal and unrelated to your actual teaching ability, which will continue to be seen as high regardless of your trembling hands or other symptoms. Therefore, it is your belief about the implications of these physiological responses that will alter your self-efficacy, rather than the sheer power of the responses themselves.

Perhaps this is the most difficult area of self-efficacy to deal with in the classroom. It has a particular relevance to those areas of the curriculum such as drama, music and sport where there are obvious performance elements. Here, students will need to be taught that feelings of nervousness or distress can be a natural reaction to stressful situations such as an assessment or performance occasion. Many high-performance athletes or musicians will say that the controlled experience of these symptoms is a boost to their performance rather than a hindrance. A positive channelling or understanding of the physiological response is possible for most students but it will take time to develop. More generally, it will be important for all teachers to frame assessment items carefully and monitor their students' responses to these occasions. This can only be helped by making assessment a natural part of the classroom routine (the key focus of strategies such as assessment for learning) rather than high-profile, one-off occasions where passing an examination becomes an imperative (which could be a particularly bad use of assessment of learning).

REFLECTIVE TASK

Think through the consequences of current assessment practices on students' sense of self-efficacy. Try to apply each of the above sources that affect self-efficacy to the design and implementation of assessment practices in your classroom. What would the models look like?

In this section we have considered a range of physical, affective and perceptual issues that will affect how you seek to implement assessment processes in your classroom. Many of these circulate around the idea that the student should be placed at the heart of the teaching, learning and assessment process. What does that mean in practice? It is to this issue that we will now turn our attention.

Motivation for learning is at the heart of assessment in the classroom

One of the greatest challenges in teaching is to maintain your students' desire to learn. How many times have you said to a fellow student or teaching colleague, student X has so much potential if only they could be more interested and apply themselves? It is essential that you get to know your students well in order to maintain this desire for learning. Assessment can have a very important role in allowing you to build up a picture of their abilities, aspirations and needs as learners.

As we have discussed above, the importance of issues such as self-esteem, self-regulation and self-efficacy all play a part here in promoting positive models of learning. Here, we are going to take a slightly different tack and consider how a student's sense of motivation for learning can be a key informant to the development of secure assessment practices in the classroom.

RESEARCH SUMMARY RESEARCH SUMMARY **RESEARCH SUMMARY** RESEARCH SUMMARY

Intrinsic and extrinsic motivation

Within the research literature on motivation in education, there are normally two forms of motivation that are routinely discussed: intrinsic and extrinsic motivation.

Intrinsic motivation is the desire to carry out an activity for the sake of the activity itself. Amabile's research on intrinsic motivation is interesting (Amabile, 1989). According to her research, intrinsic motivation has three main requirements.

1. Interest
This is relatively obvious, but anyone is more likely to be motivated by something that has captured their interest rather than being of no perceived value.

2. Competence
The motivating effects of increasing competence in a particular domain are considerable. Students will seek out activities and persist in them for longer if they feel they are mastering something, particularly if they are doing this on their own. (Amablie, 1989, in Starko, 2001, p143)

3. Self-determination
This moves students beyond the need for success in a particular activity. To be intrinsically motivated, they have to feel that they are pursuing the activity because they have chosen to do so. They have to feel that they are working on an activity, in a particular subject area, for their own reasons rather than for yours (Amabile, 1989 in Starko, 2001, p144).

Intrinsic motivation is contrasted with extrinsic motivation. Within the context of this chapter, which is focusing on the development of assessment practice in the classroom, extrinsic motivation could be associated with external rewards such as you praising your students, giving out prizes for successful work, grading work against set criteria, positive testing or even the avoidance of punishments. The research literature seems to suggest that the use of extrinsic motivation can only shape students' behaviour so much. Its overuse can lead to conformity to a teacher's expected outcomes which, of course, is necessary to receive the award. In this context, conformity becomes the opposite of creativity. This may or may not be desirable depending on the particular outcome.

Relatively recent research has begun to explore a more positive interpretation of extrinsic motivation in the classroom. Eisenberger and Armeli's work (1997) has shown that extrinsic rewards can lead to 'enduring improvements even in a creative area such as music when children were rewarded for specific "creative" behaviours such as incorporating unexpected elements or producing alternative possibilities' (Cropley, 2001, p62).

Both models of intrinsic and extrinsic motivation need to be used to underpin your model of assessment in the classroom. There is a clear balance needed between these two particular types of motivation. But the general issue is clear: the teacher holds the keys to motivation.

REFLECTIVE TASK

Spend some time thinking back on a recent lesson that you have taught. Were the themes of interest, competence and self-determination evident in your lesson plan or in the interactions within the lesson? If so, what impact did they have on the students' learning? If not, how could you seek to build them into future lessons? Finally, what do you think the correct balance is between extrinsic and intrinsic motivation in your subject area?

Models of assessment that exhibit certain attributes can helpfully ensure that students remain motivated throughout your lessons. Chapman and King (2005, pp 23–6) helpfully examine a number of these that we will use here as a starting point.

Firstly, you need to beware of students' level of concern about a particular assessment process. If student motivation is low, negative attitudes may come to the fore and you will need to plan for successful learning experiences in order to boost their confidence and develop an internal desire to succeed. You could do this through the provision of mastery experiences, vicarious learning opportunities or social persuasion. If the expectations placed on an individual student are too high, this may also cause them to be anxious and not perform to the peak of their ability. In this scenario, you may need to counsel and reassure a student as to the specific purpose or function of a particular piece of assessment and the consequences that will flow from it into future learning. Chapman and King suggest that it is possible to observe and assess attitudes and feelings that a student brings to a particular assessment task. Their table of 'Engagement–disengagement spectrum of feelings and responses' gives us a helpful insight into some of the more obvious behaviours that students might exhibit in response to a piece of assessment:

Feelings	Possible observed reactions
No desire to engage in assessment. 1. I am not going to do this. 2. I would rather not do this. 3. I do not want to do this. 4. I'll just do the easy parts. 5. I will do enough to stay out of trouble. 6. I have to complete this because it is required. 7. I understand, and I am going to do this. 8. I am excited about doing my very best on this work. *Great desire to engage in assessment.*	Does not do it. Does something else. Exhibits a negative attitude. Completes a few parts. Tasks are incomplete. Does enough to get by. Completes it to the best of their ability. Does the best work possible. Goes the extra mile.

(After Chapman and King, 2005, p24)

Secondly, encouraging students' motivation for learning is helped when you are aware of what your students are doing, thinking and learning at each stage of a lesson. As we will discuss in Chapter 9, the recording of assessment is dependent on you developing a perceptive eye and ear to events in your classroom. Good, critical observation of learning in the classroom is a skill which it may take time for you to develop. But it gets better with practice.

We suggest that the issue of building on students' motivation for learning and engagement in assessment goes beyond the classroom. Thirdly, effective teachers take an interest in their students' lives outside the classroom. They are aware, in a general sense, of the latest fads, trends, hobbies and pastimes that young people have. They are able to converse, when appropriate, about these things and bring examples from contemporary culture into their teaching. They bring learning to life through an engagement with the world outside the classroom and attempt to illustrate a broad sweep of intellectual engagement through the juxtaposition of curriculum requirements and National Curriculum topics with real-life examples. In a general sense this will engage the majority of students and allow them to develop a coherent understanding of the learning in light of a wider understanding of cultural, political, social or other issues.

Fourthly, and perhaps most importantly, it will be vital that you build an atmosphere in your classroom that celebrates learning and encourages positive responses to assessment, whether formative or summative. It is self-evident that motivated students will perform at their best and utilise their knowledge, skills and understanding to do well in particular tasks. Promoting a positive, can-do environment for learning is essential. This can be done in numerous ways. Perhaps the most important is through the use of encouraging comments and positive body language that you adopt in your teaching role. Try to avoid put-downs and sarcasm. Even done in humorous ways, these can leave their mark on students. Be a teacher who smiles, someone who acknowledges good work or effort through a simple thumbs-up or nod of the head. Make an effort to praise students more than criticise them. Lead and encourage a classroom culture in which success breeds success and which all are valued. This may take time. But it is worth it. As well as creating opportunities in which you can assess students naturally and simply, it will lead to them being better behaved, motivated and give them a chance to shine.

Assessment and teaching: symbiotic processes

As we have been considering throughout this book, the processes of assessment are very closely linked to the processes of teaching and learning. Chapter 1 presented you with the following diagrammatic representation of how assessment fits into a model of teaching and learning.

Figure 7.1 Assessment within teaching and learning

We have also emphasised the importance of constructing a routine of assessment in which the collection and analysis of assessment data become part of a reflective cycle. This will not only give you the information you need about your students' learning but will also provide you with useful data about the effectiveness of your teaching. In this practical sense, the assessment of your students and the development of effective teaching is a symbiotic process. They rely upon each other and can usually inform each other with positive consequences for you and your students.

In the final part of this chapter that has focused on using assessment in the classroom, we will briefly explore this symbiotic relationship in more detail. We will give some examples of how processes of assessment can link closely with more general aspects of your teaching practice, thereby illustrating how this relationship can be formed and developed. This will build on the integrated model of classroom assessment related to your planning, construction of activities and processes of review and evaluation that we explored in Chapter 5.

The *Inside the Black Box* (Black and Wiliam, 1998) research provides a useful backdrop to this issue. It has been cited and used as part of a government guide to Assessment for Learning (DfES, 2002, pp19–39). A summary of the main findings is provided below.

RESEARCH SUMMARY RESEARCH SUMMARY **RESEARCH SUMMARY** RESEARCH SUMMARY

Inside the Black Box (Black and Wiliam, 1998) is a really helpful and influential piece of work that summarises the main findings from a number of studies on assessment from around the world. Its findings have influenced government publications on assessment, including the Key Stage 3 National Strategy. *Inside the Black Box* identifies five simple principles that can help you improve your students' learning through assessment.

1. Provide effective feedback to students.
2. Actively involve your students in their own learning.
3. Adjust your teaching to take account of the results of assessment.
4. Recognise the profound influence assessment has on the motivation and self-esteem of students, both of which are crucial to learning.
5. Consider the need for students to be able to assess themselves and to understand how to improve.

But there are risks that the research identifies in respect of assessment. It could be possible that you will:

- **value quantity and presentation rather than the quality of your students' learning;**
- **lower the self-esteem of students by over-concentrating on judgements rather than advice for improvement;**
- **demoralise students by comparing them negatively and repeatedly with more successful learners;**
- **give feedback which serves social and managerial purposes rather than helping students to learn more effectively;**
- **work with an insufficient picture of students' learning needs.**

In conclusion, the *Inside the Black Box* research project drew a number of conclusions about what characterises good assessment for learning. Successful assessment for learning:

- **is embedded in a view of teaching and learning of which it is an essential part;**
- **involves sharing learning goals with students;**
- **aims to help students to know and to recognise the standards they are aiming for;**
- **involves students in self-assessment;**
- **provides feedback which leads to students recognising their next steps and how to take them;**
- **involves both the teacher and students reviewing, and reflecting on, assessment information.**

Within this research summary, you will notice our themes of assessment as an integrated part of teaching and learning. Let's explore how this works practically for each of our three examples: planning, teaching activities and review/evaluation.

Assessment as an integrated part of planning

Make sure that you have assessment in mind from the very first point of your planning for an individual lesson. Whatever assessment strategy you are going to use – formative, summative, peer or self-assessment – ensure that your lesson plan provides you with opportunities for some kind of assessment activity however simple or routine.

Having planned your lesson, use that planning to frame the opportunities for assessment with your students. Make sure that you tell them what the learning objectives are for the lesson and how you are going to facilitate their progress and support their work. How will they know that they have achieved what you desired? What are the markers or indicators of success that you are expecting to see? At the early stage of a lesson, these things can be communicated simply and quickly. Some schools have a policy of writing learning objectives on the board and students have to write them down into a planner or exercise book. This may be appropriate in some cases. But either way, they need to be discussed, shared and brought to life in a meaningful way for students.

Finally, you will need to ensure that your planning in respect of learning objectives and outcomes is personalised for each student. There are a number of techniques for doing this and we will discuss these further, including how you differentiate your teaching materials for assessment purposes, in the next chapter. But at a general level, students will respond as individuals to the work you have set. They need to be aware of how your general planning relates to them specifically. And this isn't just about meeting the needs of those students with SEN or on the Gifted and Talented register. Your assessment practice should build in a process of individual target setting for each student. The monitoring of these targets can be done in different ways. Personalisation of the curriculum is a very important current theme in education and assessment practices have an important role to play here.

Assessment as an integrated part of teaching activities

Assessment should be an increasingly common part in the design and implementation of your teaching activities. As we discussed above, this might be in the way that you construct these activities to allow students' self-efficacy to increase as they experience successful completion. Teaching activities can include elements of peer and self-assessment that allow students to reflect and evaluate their work in progress. This will provide useful insights for you. Perhaps there are opportunities for you to provide a greater degree of personalisation within teaching activities so that students can tailor the activity and explore areas of particular individual interest. While not appropriate in every situation, these opportunities sometimes allow students to become intrinsically motivated and take a greater degree of responsibility for their own learning.

Assessment as an integrated part of review and evaluation

Assessment has a very important role to play in forming strategies of review and evaluation within your lessons. This has a number of dimensions that will be introduced here and explored in greater detail in Chapter 8.

The feedback that you give to students will be vital in helping them recognise what they have achieved, what their next learning steps will be and how they should take them. The literature shows that students value oral as well as written feedback on their work. This feedback should take place at different stages within a lesson and be given to individuals and to groups of students. Feedback should be positive and constructive but not patronising. As we have seen, praise for the sake of praise can have a detrimental effect. It needs to be grounded in reality, in what the student has achieved (however small that might be in some cases) and authentic in its expression. The identification and positive reinforcement of small learning steps enables students to see that they are making progress and will build their sense of self-esteem in your subject area.

Conclusion

Involving students in the review and evaluation of the assessment data that you are collecting will have a positive impact on their perception of what assessment is for. Shared ownership of the data and the process can only be a good thing here. It demystifies assessment and results in students sharing your model of assessment as an integrated part of the teaching and learning process. Providing time in your lessons for this process is vital. We will be considering the role of the plenary in Chapter 8 as one strategy for encouraging this process. Throughout your lessons, encourage students to be reflective about their work through the careful use of questioning (as we considered in Chapter 4).

PRACTICAL TASK PRACTICAL TASK PRACTICAL TASK PRACTICAL TASK PRACTICAL TASK

In this final section we have considered how assessment should be integrated within general processes of teaching and learning. We have explored some specific issues including:

- **the planning of learning objectives and learning outcomes;**
- **the design and delivery of teaching activities;**
- **the importance of feedback;**
- **involving students in processes of review and evaluation.**

Think about a lesson that you are going to teach in the near future. For each of these issues, identify one specific way in which you are going to develop your teaching. Your new approach should lead to a change in your practice that gives you a new method or focus for assessment. Having taught the lesson, evaluate the consequences of your choices and make modifications for the future practice.

A SUMMARY OF **KEY POINTS**

> **The classroom atmosphere will have a direct impact on your students' chances of learning successfully.**

> **Take care of your classroom's physical environment, ensuring that it promotes the learning atmosphere you want to develop.**

> **Construct a positive affective domain that will enhance students' emotional response to learning and develop their emotional intelligence.**

> **Generating your students' self-efficacy is a key to creating a positive classroom atmosphere for assessment.**

> **Extrinsic and intrinsic motivation both have a part to play in underpinning models of classroom assessment.**

> **Assessment and teaching are symbiotic processes that usefully inform each other and, when conceptualised as such, result in a unified model of teaching in which teachers and students work together for common ends.**

REFERENCES REFERENCES **REFERENCES** REFERENCES REFERENCES REFERENCES

Amabile, T. (1989) *Growing up creative.* New York: Crown.

Bandura, R. (1997) *Self-efficacy: the exercise of control*. New York: WH Freeman and Company.

Black, P. and Wiliam, D. (1998) *Inside the black box: raising standards through classroom assessment.* London: King's College.

Chapman, C. and King, R. (2005) *Differentiated assessment strategies: one tool doesn't fit all.* Thousand Oaks, Calif.: Corwin Press, Inc.

Cropley, A. (2001) *Creativity in education and learning: a guide for teachers and educators*. London: Kogan Page.

DfES (2002) *Key Stage 3 National Strategy: Training materials for the foundation subjects.* London: DfES.

Eisenberger, R. and Armeli, S. (1997) Can salient reward increase creative performance without reducing intrinsic creative interest? *Journal of Personality and Social Psychology*, 72: 652–63.

Goleman, D. (1998) *Working with emotional intelligence*. New York: Bantam Books.

Ormrod, J.E. (2006) *Educational psychology: developing learners* (5th ed.). New Jersey: J. Merrill. Companion website: **http://wps.prenhall.com/chet_ormrod_edpsych_5/0,5159,1774689-,00.html** (accessed 18 June 2007)

Starko, A. (2001) *Creativity in the classroom.* London and New Jersey: Lawrence Erlbaum Associates.

FURTHER READING FURTHER READING **FURTHER READING** FURTHER READING

Black, P. and Wiliam, D. (1998) *Inside the black box: raising standards through classroom assessment.* London: King's College.

Chapman, C. and King, R. (2005) *Differentiated assessment strategies: one tool doesn't fit all.* Thousand Oaks, Calif.: Corwin Press, Inc.

DfES (2002) *Key Stage 3 National Strategy: Training materials for the foundation subjects.* London: DfES.

8
Valuing the student role in assessment

Chapter objectives

By the end of this chapter you should:

- **understand how students should be placed at the heart of assessment practices in your classroom;**
- **appreciate the changing functions of assessment types and how different assessment processes facilitate or inhibit students' involvement;**
- **develop an understanding of the potential benefits for actively including students in classroom assessment processes;**
- **continue to develop your understanding of how assessment and teaching go hand in hand and how the students' role in assessment will impact on all areas of your pedagogy;**
- **analyse student-centred assessment processes such as peer assessment, self-assessment, ipsative assessment and computer-assisted assessment and consider their various benefits for expanding models of classroom assessment.**

Professional Standards for QTS

This chapter will help you to meet the following Professional Standards for QTS:
Q11, Q12, Q26, Q27, Q28, Q29

Introduction

This book has taken a very practical look at the use of assessment in teaching and learning within the secondary curriculum. It has challenged you to think about assessment as an integrated part of your teaching and learning. It has drawn on a range of recent research about assessment and translated this into concepts and ideas which should help you develop your classroom teaching in such a way that both empowers you, as a teacher, and provides good learning opportunities for your students.

In this chapter, we turn to the vital role that students have in assessment. As we will see, their role is varied and interesting. Fostering their interest in assessment and how it can help them improve their learning will be a crucial element of your teaching strategy.

In order to understand the importance of placing students and their interests at the centre of a teaching strategy, it is worth taking a longer view of assessment in education for a moment. After all, it was not always the case that students were conceptualised as being an important part of an assessment process. Assessment was once something that was done to students. Getting them involved, in any meaningful way, would have been thought of as strange by educators early in the twentieth century. Falchikov presents an interesting summary of these developments (Falchikov, 2005, pp83–5). She observes that it was really only from the late 1950s that teachers began to consider including students in the process of assessment and analysing, in a meaningful way, their role within it. Throughout the later part of the twentieth century the inclusion of students into the processes and methodologies of assessment became more common. By the time we reach the 1990s the benefits of involving students in assessment are widely reported in the research literature. However, there is a corresponding burden that accompanies this development: the increasing size of classes and the associated burden of assessment. This is also matched by the burgeoning external pressures on teachers in terms of accountability from senior managers and other external agents, not least politicians.

RESEARCH SUMMARY RESEARCH SUMMARY **RESEARCH SUMMARY** RESEARCH SUMMARY

A survey of student roles in assessment

More generally, the changing nature of assessment and students' involvement within it, is charted by Serafini (2000) and Pearson *et al.* (2001). Serafini identifies three main stages, to which Pearson adds a fourth. These stages are briefly summarised below.

1. Assessment as measurement

Traditional assessment as a form of measurement focuses on norm-referenced standardised testing. Within this model, issues such as objectivity and reliability take preference over other things such as student involvement. Birenbaum (1996) goes so far as to equate this form of assessment as corresponding to the concept of the student as an empty vessel into which knowledge is poured and measured.

2. Assessment as procedure

Here, the focus is on the assessment procedure rather than the defining of any particular assessment purpose. While this approach might include the use of a range of qualitative approaches to the collection of data (a topic to which we will return in Chapter 9), the preoccupation with method has led some (Daly, in Serafini 2000, pp2–3) to describe this approach as 'methodolatry' and 'an overemphasis on the correct method of doing things, rather than on the purposes for doing those things'. As in the previous stage, students are inactive within this process. Obviously, assessment as procedure is something that only engages teachers in any meaningful way.

3. Assessment as enquiry

In this stage, Serafini argues that students become involved in the assessment process. This approach incorporates a wide variety of assessment devices and methods and is accompanied by teachers redefining and extending their traditional teaching role in a number of ways. Birenbaum and Dochy (1996, p7) see this culture of assessment as emphasising a number of particular features, including:

- **an integration of assessment with instruction;**

- **assessment of learning processes rather than learning products;**

- **evaluation of a student's individual progress relative to his or her own starting point.**

4. Assessment as quality control

Pearson *et al.* (2001) add a fourth stage to Serafini's three-part model. This is a stage that all teachers will recognise: assessment as quality control. This has at least two components. Firstly, external pressures on schools for assessment data have grown immensely in the last ten years. Secondly, the internal pressures on individual teachers from their senior management teams have increased accordingly. In either case, it seems clear that within assessment as a form of quality control, teachers and students seem to lose influence over what is assessed, when it is assessed and how it is assessed. Boud goes as far as arguing that:

> *Accountability and portrayal of accomplishments is clearly important, but in the process of giving attention to certification we have pushed into the background a concern for learning and the necessary assessment processes which need to accompany it.*

> (Boud 2000, p156)

Clearly, it is going to be an important part of your role as a teacher to ensure that your students' learning is placed as the number one priority in your work. Issues of quality control and quality assurance are undoubtedly important but they should not be allowed to distract you from your main teaching role and how you conceptualise the process of assessment and the students' role within it.

REFLECTIVE TASK

Think about the roles that students might play in assessment processes. Which of the above models best reflects classroom practice that you have observed recently? Which model would you seek to aspire to in your own teaching? Which model embraces the student most wholeheartedly? Is there evidence of this in the teaching you have observed?

What about issues of quality control? How are they formed and shaped within the school you are in? What type of information is demanded from teachers by assessment co-ordinators or senior management teams? Do teachers feel a conflict between the collection of these data types and more classroom-based or student-focused assessment strategies? Is there an integration or a disintegration of assessment practice at this level?

Perhaps it is obvious, but this book has taken 'assessment as enquiry' as its main philosophical position. But why should we be so concerned about valuing the student's role within assessment? In probably the most comprehensive survey of reported reasons for including students within assessment, Falchikov (2005, pp87–107) identifies the following reasons in order of frequency:

- **improving student learning and development;**
- **facilitating students' acquisition and development of skills, knowledge and understanding;**
- **pressure from external and internal bodies;**
- **measuring reliability or validity;**
- **addressing problems;**
- **investigating the process of assessment;**
- **developing students' communication skills;**
- **transferring power from teacher to student;**
- **the need to provide feedback to students;**
- **saving time and reducing teacher workload;**
- **dissemination and application of ideas.**

PRACTICAL TASK PRACTICAL TASK PRACTICAL TASK PRACTICAL TASK PRACTICAL TASK

What proportion of a typical lesson does a teacher spend carrying out student-centred assessment practices? Try the following simple experiment.

During a lesson observation in your subject, use the above indicators as a framework to note down the occasions when the teacher utilises an approach that involves the students directly in assessment. The table below can be used to monitor your responses.

Student-centred assessment indicators	Frequency	Notes
Using assessment directly to improve a student's learning or developing their skills, knowledge or understanding		
Measuring students' skills, knowledge or understanding		

Checking students' skills, knowledge or understanding against other previously collected data		
Developing students' communication skills through the assessment process		
Giving the students power over the nature, mode and extent of the assessment process		
Providing feedback to the students		
Using assessment to help students address problems in their learning		

Turning to consider the Professional Standards for Qualified Teacher Status, we find resonances with many of these ideas applied towards your own development as a teacher. It is worth reminding yourself of the main section from these standards that deals with assessment:

Assessing, monitoring and giving feedback

Q26 (a) Make effective use of a range of assessment, monitoring and recording strategies.

   (b) Assess the learning needs of those they teach in order to set challenging learning objectives.

Q27 Provide timely, accurate and constructive feedback on learners' attainment, progress and areas for development.

Q28 Support and guide learners to reflect on their learning, identify the progress they have made and identify their emerging learning needs.

Reviewing teaching and learning

Q29 Evaluate the impact of their teaching on the progress of all learners, and modify their planning and classroom practice where necessary.

(TDA, 2007)

We are going to take two main themes from these standards to frame the application of ideas about valuing the students' role in assessment directly to your teaching. Firstly, we are going to consider how valuing the students' role in assessment affects general classroom teaching. This will address Q26(a) and Q29 specifically. Secondly, we are going to consider how a range of student-centred approaches to assessment can be usefully adopted to help personalise learning to meet standards Q26(b), Q27 and Q28.

Effective assessment with the student role in mind

Our argument throughout the book has been that teaching and assessment go hand in hand. You could say that is impossible to do one well without the other. Valuing the students' role in assessment will therefore implicate all of your teaching throughout a given lesson. We are going to explore some examples of this by briefly analysing some generic teaching skills and concepts: explaining, modelling and plenaries. For each of these, we will consider how they can help us involve and value the students' role in assessment.

Explaining

How do you explain things to students? What are the characteristics of a successful explanation? What are the key things that students need to understand or know in order for an explanation to be successful?

For a forthcoming lesson, write down your explanation for a new concept that you are going to introduce. Analyse your explanation and try to identify key explanatory themes or devices that you have used to make it effective.

Almost every lesson that you teach will have a period of explanation at some point. Explaining things is a skill that can be learnt, practised and developed. Effective explanations are underpinned by a range of techniques including:

- **having a key concept or idea which is at the core of the explanation;**
- **using a hook that grabs students' interest and attention;**
- **varying your language, intonation and posture to emphasise key points;**
- **signposting statements that signal new directions or summarise key learning;**
- **humour, which may or may not come naturally, and can help key ideas remain in students' minds;**
- **examples that illustrate key concepts and establish understanding;**
- **connecting new ideas to students' previous experiences or existing knowledge;**
- **props that add power and illustration to your explanation.**

Even through a generally teacher-dominated part of the lesson such as an explanation, you can value the student role in assessment if you think through some basic questions and reflect on your response.

Reflect on the lesson that you taught within which you delivered the explanation that you wrote for the previous task. Ask yourself the following questions.

Were the key points in your explanation linked to the learning objectives of the lesson? Did you mention this to students?
Where were the students sitting during the explanation?
What were they doing?
Were you able to actively involve the students during the explanation?
Did you use any technical vocabulary during the explanation? Did you define new terms? How did you do this?
Did you ask the students any questions during the explanation? What type of questions did you use?
Did you check the students' understanding of the new concept that you had explained? When did you do this? How did you do this?
How did you link, check or reinforce the key points in your explanation throughout the rest of the lesson? What outcomes did the students demonstrate in their work that proved to you that the explanation had been successful or otherwise?

Through completing the above tasks, we hope that you have seen how explanations, when linked to the larger context of a particular lesson, can really be used to value the student role in assessment. Explanations need not be a monologue in which you struggle through something that you prepared earlier. They can be dynamic, entertaining and inclusive if you think through how students will not only receive new knowledge or information, but also process this through the rest of the lesson. Much of this comes down to effective planning in which your learning objectives and outcomes for a particular lesson are skilfully linked to how you present new information. Other key skills in explanation relate to your use of spoken language, your ability to empathise with students, to ask skilful questions about the process of their learning (maybe even within the explanatory phase) and conceptualise your explanation as part of the larger opportunity for learning that the lesson represents. Ultimately, valuing the student role in assessment through effective explanations comes down to tracing your engagement with students and their learning throughout a whole lesson. But the explanatory phase of most lessons holds an important key for future learning and it will be vital that you obtain a clear picture of how students respond to this phase of the lesson before you can move on.

Modelling

Linked to explanations, modelling can be a very effective teaching strategy. When students are going to learn a new skill it is often helpful if they can see it being done by someone else, perhaps with that person thinking aloud about what they are doing and explaining why they are making the choices. This can give students the opportunity to ask questions about the process and can give you, the teacher, the opportunity to reiterate certain stages of the process if you feel that students need some kind of reinforcement. We would suggest that modelling is a vital part in nearly every lesson.

Done well, modelling has a particularly important role in improving students' sense of self-efficacy. As we saw in Chapter 7, if a student can see someone else, i.e. another student, succeed at a particular task then their sense of self-efficacy will be enhanced. Of course, this can work the other way around.

So, involving students in the modelling phase of a lesson can be a very helpful strategy. It can be used to positively reinforce the learning experience for all students and will raise the sense of self-efficacy for some. However, it will be important to ensure that modelling, like explanations, is underpinned by some good strategies that integrate the opportunities for student involvement in assessment alongside the wider teaching and learning issues.

REFLECTIVE TASK

Reflect on a lesson that you have observed or taught in which modelling was part of the teacher's or your pedagogy. Ask yourself the following questions as an aid to your reflection and as a way of thinking through how modelling can help value the students' role in assessment.

How did the modelling of the new idea or process link to the learning objectives of the lesson? Were these explicit to students and were they able to relate them together? What strategies did you adopt to encourage this process and what evidence do you have that it worked?

Were you able to actively involve the students in the modelling process? If so, were they successful and was there any evidence of other students' self-efficacy increasing?

How did you check the students' understanding of the new concept that you had modelled? When did you do this? How did you do this?

How did you link, check or reinforce the key points demonstrated in your modelling throughout the rest of the lesson? Did students simply copy what you did? Did they have to extend this in any way?

Were the outcomes of the modelling differentiated in any way to support students' different educational needs?

What outcomes did the students demonstrate in their work that proved to you that the modelling had been successful or otherwise?

Plenaries

In recent years, plenaries have become recognised as a very useful strategy for teachers as a way of developing and valuing the students' role in assessment. While the summing up of learning objectives, the analysis of learning outcomes and the signposting of new learning was undoubtedly an effective teaching strategy long before the various National Strategies were implemented, the adoption of these strategies in primary and secondary education have seen a huge increase in the use of plenary sessions in all subjects. Normally these take place at the end of lessons, although there is good evidence that their use throughout lessons can really encourage and facilitate learning. According to one set of National Strategy materials (DfES, 2002, p193), plenaries have many characteristics. They:

- **draw together the whole group;**
- **summarise and take stock of learning so far;**
- **consolidate and extend the learning;**
- **direct students to the next stage of learning;**
- **occur at strategic moments in the teaching sequence;**
- **often occur at the end of lessons but can occur at other points in the lesson;**
- **highlight not only what students learn, but how they learn;**
- **help to determine the next steps in learning.**

The key thing that we want to emphasise here is that to run an effective plenary you have to place the students' learning experiences at the heart of the dialogue. Plenaries become problematic when the teacher remains in control, talks too much, simply repeats the learning objectives that were established at the beginning of the lesson or does not communicate the purpose of the plenary to the students.

Effective plenaries place the student at the heart of the assessment process if you are able to adopt some of the following simple principles.

1. Give students prior knowledge of the plenary and the type of questions that you are going to be asking.
2. Extend the feedback that students give you by using supplementary or extension questions. Try to avoid low-level reiteration of basic ideas. (For more help with questioning please see Chapter 4.)
3. Ensure that the plenary continues to progress the learning rather than solely summarise it. Key signposting of future learning (e.g. ideas in the next lesson) can help to motivate students and sustain their interest.
4. Try to vary the routine of your plenaries. They don't always have to be questions and answers. Think about those visual and kinaesthetic learners in the class. Try to be imaginative in the structure and process of plenary sessions.
5. Develop a conceptual map of the plenary for your own assessment purposes and to remind students what has been learnt in subsequent lessons. The use of an interactive whiteboard can do this very effectively because you can save the map for future use.

Using the five points above, plan a plenary session for a forthcoming lesson. In particular, think very carefully about the type of questions you are going to ask (including supplementary questions) and how you are going to 'map' the outcomes of the plenary in such a way that helps students make sense of their learning and gives you some assessment data. To help with this, refer back to our discussions of questioning in Chapter 4, particularly the list of question stems in Table 4.1 Having taught the lesson, reflect on the plenary and identify it strengths, weaknesses and areas for future development.

Student-centred assessment processes

As we have seen, valuing the student role in assessment will affect your teaching at a fundamental level. It will cause you to think about the various elements of a lesson and how they are delivered. If assessment is truly a holistic element of an effective pedagogy, then it will infiltrate through to all areas and affect how we explain, model and question students. Now, we are going to turn our attention to some specific student-centred assessment processes that you could adopt in your classroom. Each of them has pros and cons. You will need to develop your knowledge and understanding about each one and how they might suit particular teaching situations.

We are going to examine briefly four of the most common types of student-centred assessment processes: peer assessment, self-assessment, ipsative assessment and computer-assisted assessment. You will remember that peer and self-assessment were introduced in Chapter 4. Here, we will not revisit all of the arguments and issues that were presented earlier. Rather, we will briefly make a justification for them as student-centred assessment processes before moving on the remaining two new student-centred assessment processes.

Peer and self-assessment

As we have seen, peer assessment involves students assessing the performance of other students. It is often used in assessing group work. On most occasions teachers use peer assessment to assess the product of a piece of group work, e.g. a piece of writing, a musical performance or an artwork. However, there is no reason why this cannot be extended to include the process by which a piece of work has been produced. In fact, the process of how a piece of work has been completed is probably more visible to the members of a group than it is to the teacher. Allowing group members to assess each other may well produce a more interesting account of the educational processes than can be obtained via other student-centred methods. The criteria by which a peer assessment is conducted could either be established by the teacher, the student, or via a negotiation. This should be done prior to the adoption of the peer assessment in a particular lesson. Setting criteria for peer assessment in advance can be a very helpful way to reinforce, and on occasions develop, learning objectives that you might have set for a lesson.

Self-assessment is very closely related to peer assessment and involves students assessing their own performance. This has one obvious benefit: it saves you time. However, there is a better educational justification for self-assessment, namely that the process of self-assessment is, in itself, an inherently valuable and worthy learning experience. If education is about empowering the student and, eventually, one that should lead to their independence as learners, then self-assessment will have an important role to play in the secondary curriculum. Many teachers worry that students will be too lenient on themselves. This is not necessarily true and there are many studies that show this not to be the case. Regardless, there are a number of safeguards to prevent this happening, not least the opportunity of using self-assessment alongside other techniques to provide a measure of counterbalance through a process of triangulation.

One of the most obvious and powerful benefits of self-assessment is that it links very clearly to processes of professional development which underpin many vocational and academic courses in further or higher education. The process of reflection, which is an essential characteristic of professional development planning, can be developed through self-assessment practices in the classroom by simple mechanisms such as getting students to keep a reflective account of their learning for a set period of time, engaging them in ongoing evaluation questions about their learning and the setting of targets for their learning (weekly or from one scheme of work to another).

Ipsative assessment

The original Latin derivation of 'ipsative' is 'of the self'. This gives a clue to the practice of ipsative assessment, which relates to how students assess their present performance against their prior performance in a related area. This can be effective for a number of reasons. It can allow students to clearly monitor their progress and make sense of the curriculum in a very personal way. It can also help reinforce their knowledge of, and development in, key skills within your subject. It can helpfully give students a real sense of progress over the longer term of a key stage.

Ultimately, the practice of ipsative assessment will be facilitated by the structure of the curriculum that is offered to the students. As we saw in Chapter 2, the spiral curriculum is the obvious example of a curriculum structure that will facilitate a natural process of ipsative assessment. This is reproduced in Figure 8.1.

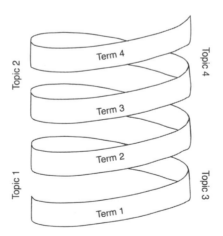

Figure 8.1 The spiral curriculum model

This model, which is often attributed to the early work of Bruner (1960), has many attractive features. Not least is its underpinning notion of a clear structure to learning that revisits key ideas. It can be communicated simply to students through effective teaching. Bruner himself commented that:

The teaching and learning of structure, rather than simply the mastery of facts and techniques, is at the center of the classic problem of transfer. If earlier learning is to render later learning easier, it must do so by providing a general picture in terms of which the relations between things encountered earlier and later are made as clear as possible.

(Bruner, 1960, p12)

Two points become apparent here that are relevant to ipsative assessment. Firstly, the learning that is being observed, noted and analysed through ipsative assessment needs to be linked, explicitly, to previous learning and then, by projection, to the possibility of future learning. Secondly, learning is more than just being knowledgeable. It is about placing that knowledge within a relationship. We might call this a context for learning that spans beyond the classroom into a number of other areas. Certainly this would include prior learning, perhaps within your subject area, but would also include knowledge gained in other subject areas, students' personal interests or hobbies, and knowledge gained through participation within wider cultural groups within society.

Bruner challenges us to rethink the very purpose of our teaching. What is the ultimate aim of your teaching? Isn't it about getting students to think for themselves in the process of knowledge formation? This is how Bruner, much more elegantly, puts it:

To instruct someone. . .is not a matter of getting him to commit results to mind. Rather, it is to teach him to participate in the process that makes possible the establishment of knowledge. We teach a subject not to produce little living libraries on that subject, but rather to get a student to think mathematically for himself, to consider matters as an historian does, to take part in the process of knowledge-getting. Knowing is a process not a product.

(Bruner, 1966, p72)

Ipsative assessment can be a great way to get students to think about the process of their learning. The following task will help you to begin to experiment with this approach for your own subject area.

PRACTICAL TASK PRACTICAL TASK PRACTICAL TASK PRACTICAL TASK PRACTICAL TASK

Identify three main skills that underpin your particular subject. Examine the way in which these are currently taught and assessed, either in your own teaching or within the school where you are currently working. When and how are these key skills assessed under your current assessment arrangements?

During the next opportunity that you have to plan an extended series of lessons, ensure that at least one of these skills is taught in three different contexts throughout a sequence of lessons. On each occasion, provide a simple framework within which students can assess their progress in relation to that skill. You could provide them with a framework of criteria to assist this process. Or you could build in another process of student-centred assessment to support this ipsative cycle.

Following the second and third opportunities that students have to learn and apply this skill, conduct a similar ipsative assessment process. But on these occasions, use questioning or other devices to allow students to compare their progress from the previous assessment. Through discussion, link up their learning on each occasion and praise and encourage students as appropriate for the progress they have made. Get them to develop an individual target that relates closely to the skill being developed and build in general systems of support for students as they continue to focus their work in this particular area.

Computer-assisted assessment

In Chapter 9 we will look at some of the general uses that ICT can play in supporting the recording, storage and analysis of assessment data. At the end of that chapter, we will look at how the uses of electronic portfolios contained with generic pieces of virtual learning environment software such as Moodle or Elgg can help facilitate a sharing of assessment processes.

Computer-assisted assessment (CAA) has a slightly different focus, although there are many points of contact with general developments in electronic portfolio software. It is generally defined as:

> *The use of computers to deliver, mark and analyse assignments or examinations. It also includes the collation and analysis of data gathered from optical mark readers (OMRs).*

(CAA Centre, 2007)

We have included CAA as a type of student-centred assessment for a number of reasons, not least because it can involve students in a process of active learning, as well as just being a teacher's tool for assessing their students' knowledge. In other words, it is not something that is done to them in the 'assessment as measurement' or 'assessment as procedure' models described earlier in this chapter. It can become part of an 'assessment for enquiry' model when handled skilfully and integrated within a sequence of learning.

We anticipate that this model of assessment might be the most unfamiliar to readers of the book. For that reason, we have drawn up a list of questions about CAA and documented some answers. The following table contains answers to a range of these common questions about CAA drawn from the CAA Centre's website (CAA Centre, 2007).

How is CAA used?	Diagnostic purposes Self-assessment Formative assessment (by giving feedback to students during or after an assessment) Summative assessment
What are the pedagogical advantages of CAA?	You can monitor your students' work easily Students can monitor their own progress easily Detailed and personalised feedback can be given to the student during or after an assessment Wide ranges of topics or skills can be assessed quickly Students are learning a range of ICT skills alongside your subject You can utilise graphics, animation, video and other multimedia elements alongside more traditional text-based questions Assessments can be repeated easily by the student and their progress monitored (in an ipsative way) Adaptive testing can be used to match the assessment to a student's current ability You can provide students with clues to answers if necessary and adjust the mark scheme accordingly

What are the other advantages of CAA?	Tests mark themselves, which saves you time Large groups can be assessed quickly You can generate diagnostic reports and analyses of whole-class progress Electronic storage of marks relates well to wider implementation of electronic portfolios of student work
What are the limitations of CAA?	Construction of good tests requires skill and practice and is initially time consuming Students need ICT skills to access the tests and complete them There may be issues associated with hardware and software costs
What subjects can incorporate CAA?	The CAA survey showed that a nearly all academic subjects make use of CAA at some point. The following subjects were ranked as having the highest percentage of CAA assessment activities. • ICT • Science • Mathematics • MFL • Business and accountancy

While CAA has predominantly been an assessment practice used by those in further and higher education, there is an increasing trend emerging of schools adopting this model of assessment. This is happening in at least three ways. Firstly, through the use of specific pieces of CAA software, secondly through a range of free online tools, and finally through the use of virtual learning environment platforms and CAA features within these.

Different publishers are producing specific pieces of CAA software. As an example, consider the *Mathematics Assessment for Learning and Teaching* software (MaLT, 2007). According to the website, *MaLT* samples all aspects of mathematics from Reception to Year 9 and provides a range of functions, including:

- **standardised scores, percentiles and National Curriculum levels;**
- **year-on-year progress assessment;**
- **attainment target performance profiles;**
- **individualised formative and diagnostic feedback to students;**
- **whole-class profiles identifying weaknesses, common misconceptions and errors.**

MaLT places a great emphasis on being a formative and a summative assessment tool. It claims to maintain 'rigorous standardised assessment' while also supporting and developing formative assessment. However, the justifications for claims like these probably lie as much with how a teacher would use such a tool as within the tool itself. Off-the-shelf packages such as *MaLT* may have a part to play in formulating CAA approaches in your teaching.

There is an increasing range of free software that will help you create and develop the process of CAA. Online tools such as *Quiz Centre* (part of the Discovery School website) and 'Create a Quiz' all help you construct simple assessment frameworks that adopt the basic principles of CAA. But there are other tools that will provide an even greater degree of personalisation and ownership over CAA processes through relatively simple interfaces. We will turn our attention to one such tool that is becoming increasingly popular in education as an assessment and learning tool.

Moodle is a free, open-source virtual learning environment. Unlike its commercial competitors, Moodle has been developed quickly by its community of users and tailored specifically towards their needs. You will find it in use across the world in a vast number of colleges and universities. There is also an increasing interest by government organisations in embracing the potential of open source software such as Moodle and the reports by Becta, the government's main advisory body for ICT, have indicated many benefits (Becta, 2005).

Although Moodle is a powerful virtual learning environment, it contains elements of CAA that may be more easily accessible for the classroom teacher. In particular, it offers a flexible quiz builder with many features of CAA systems that we have been discussing. Each question can be as simple as a multiple-choice text-based question, or you can include anything else that you might normally see on a web page including images, sound, video, etc.

As well as just being used as a way to test students about their knowledge, quizzes in Moodle can serve other purposes. You can give students practice tests that allow them to have several attempts to answer a given question. You can provide feedback when they choose a wrong answer and turn the quiz into a learning experience. You can shuffle questions in a quiz or even tailor the types of questions that students will receive if you are using Moodle more regularly and building up profiles of students' work. Whatever the purpose, function or scale of the quiz, Moodle will collate results and analyse them for various trends which you will find useful as part of your ongoing assessment work.

Conclusion

Ultimately, CAA can play a very important role in valuing and developing the student role in assessment. While it is unlikely that CAA will ever completely replace more traditional methods of assessment, student-centred or otherwise, there seems no doubt that online systems of assessment, evaluation and reflection, many of which include elements of CAA, will be increasingly seen within schools over the next ten years.

A SUMMARY OF **KEY POINTS**

> **Valuing the student role in assessment has many important benefits in your overall work as a teacher.**

> **Conceptualising assessment as enquiry is the most productive model for developing a wide range of assessment processes and including students as an integrated part of your assessment strategy.**

> **The adoption of a student-centred approach to assessment will impact on all areas of your teaching, including how you explain and model things, question students and encourage their independence as learners.**

> **Traditional models of peer and self-assessment, alongside newer models of ipsative assessment and CAA, can all be used to develop a broad student-centred assessment strategy that will produce a range of assessment data that will not only help you teach better but also facilitate your students' learning.**

REFERENCES REFERENCES **REFERENCES** REFERENCES REFERENCES REFERENCES

Becta (2005) *Open source software in schools*. Coventry: Becta. **http://publications.becta.org.uk/display.cfm?resID=25907** (accessed 20 June 2007)

Birenbaum, M. (1996) Assessment 2000: towards a pluralistic approach to assessment, Birenbaum, M. and Dochy, F.J.R.C. (eds) *Alternatives in assessment of achievements, learning processes and prior knowledge*. Boston: Kluwer Academic Publishers.

Birenbaum, M. and Dochy, F.J.R.C. (eds) (1996) *Alternatives in assessment of achievements, learning processes and prior knowledge*. Boston, Mass.: Kluwer Academic Publishers.

Boud, D. (2000) Sustainable assessment: rethinking assessment for the learning society. *Studies in Continuing Education*, 22(2) 151–67.

Bruner, J.S. (1960) *The process of education*. Cambridge, Mass.: Harvard University Press.

Bruner, J.S. (1966) *Toward a theory of instruction*. Cambridge, Mass.: Belkapp Press.

CAA Centre (2007) **www.caacentre.ac.uk** (accessed 20 June 2007)

DfES (2002) *Key Stage 3 National Strategy: Training materials for the foundation subjects.* London: DfES.

Falchikov, N. (2005) *Improving assessment through student involvement.* London: Routledge.

MaLT (2007) **www.hoddertests.co.uk/tfsearch/ks3/numeracy/MaLTnew.htm** (accessed 20 June 2007)

Pearson, P.D., Vyas, S., Sensale, L..M. and Kim, Y. (2001) Making our way through the assessment and accountability maze: where do we go now? *The Clearing House*, 74(4), 175–82.

Serafini, F. (2000) Three paradigms of assessment: measurement, procedure, and enquiry. *The Reading Teacher*, 54(4).

TDA (2007) *Professional Standards for Qualified Teacher Status*. London: TDA. (**www.tda.gov.uk**) (accessed 18 June 2007)

FURTHER READING FURTHER READING **FURTHER READING** FURTHER READING

Falchikov, N. (2005) *Improving assessment through student involvement.* London: Routledge.

Filer, A. and Pollard, A. (2000) *Social world of student assessment*. London: Continuum.

Roberts, T.S. (2006) *Self, peer and group assessment in e-learning*. London: Information Science Publishing.

9
Recording assessment

Chapter objectives

By the end of this chapter you should:

- **understand the processes of recording assessment data, including their collection, storage, interpretation and analysis;**
- **be familiar with a range of generic and specific tools that can help you record assessment data more easily;**
- **have a broader appreciation of the range of potential assessment data that can usefully be recorded.**

Professional Standards for QTS

This chapter will help you to meet the following Professional Standards for QTS: Q17, Q26b, Q27

Introduction

Classrooms are busy, complicated environments. They are full of students, resources, furniture, displays and, of course, you – the teacher. Assessment is part of this rich environment. It exists as part of your deliberate strategy to develop your students' learning through a sophisticated, meaningful and deliberate teaching practice. Assessment is embedded in your pedagogy. For that reason, processes of assessment become quite personal and, although it is right and proper that we learn from those around us, you will need to think carefully about how the assessment approaches discussed in this book will fit within your emerging pedagogy as a trainee teacher.

However you are going to conceptualise assessment within your teaching, you will be dealing with information or data about students' learning. These data will take a range of forms. Sometimes they will be written, sometimes verbal, sometimes graphical, artistic or musical and sometimes they may even be a fleeting visual snapshot of a student's body language or response that you note from the corner of your eye! The obvious questions are: what are you going to do with all this information? How can you collect, collate and make sense of this range of data and use them constructively to improve your teaching and, hopefully, your students' learning? How can you ensure that the recording of assessment information or data does not take over your teaching but remains in its place, as subservient to, and supportive of, your pedagogy?

PRACTICAL TASK PRACTICAL TASK PRACTICAL TASK PRACTICAL TASK PRACTICAL TASK

Can you categorise the various 'types' of assessment data that give evidence of students' learning? Having done so, during your next few lessons of observation or teaching try to collect or make a mental note of an example of each type. How could each 'type' be collected and stored most efficiently?

This chapter will be divided into two main sections. In the first section we will consider some practical ideas about how to collect and store assessment data. We will briefly explore ways of interpreting and analysing the information that you have collected. Finally, we will consider how you might use your data for presenting conclusions to senior managers in your school and, perhaps more importantly, how you can use them to help plan more effectively for your own teaching.

In the second section, we will be consider some of the tools – both hardware and software – that can help you manage the process of recording assessment more effectively.

The processes of recording assessment

Collecting and storing assessment data

Teachers utilise many different approaches for collecting and storing assessment data. The important point here is that the method of collection and storage should relate to the type of data that have been collected. We will give a range of examples below.

Perhaps the simplest example of this important principle is the classic weekly spelling test. Scored out of 10 or 20, the test provided a simple range of data that could be easily collected by the teacher. The data reflected how well the student spelt a range of words and, done week-by-week, perhaps gave an indication of their progress in spelling the set lists of words. The data could be easily stored in a mark book or electronically in a spreadsheet. We could agree that the collection and storage of such simple numerical data is relatively unproblematic.

Let us consider a more difficult scenario. In this classroom, students are engaged in a design task. They are learning about electronic circuitry through a hands-on, practical exercise in which they have to design and produce a simple 'point of sale' interface. Working in groups of three, they are connecting together light bulbs, buzzers, batteries and various other bits of equipment, soldering connections and testing circuits. In previous lessons they have worked on concept drawings and generated various hypotheses about their interface. During today's lesson, the classroom is full of students chattering about their work. Their discussions are full of challenges and assertions about each other's ideas, value judgements about the effectiveness of their work, gentle ribbing of each other when things don't go quite as expected and the occasional flare-up when things get a little too heated.

Imagine your role within this classroom. You circulate around the room and observe. You eavesdrop on a range of student conversations. Perhaps you are asked for your opinion about a particular design choice. Do you give a direct answer? Perhaps you are elusive and skilfully direct students' thinking along a new path. You observe their design work in process, including the errors and poor choices as well as the effective and polished responses. You observe students interacting with each other. You mentally note who seems to be taking the lead in a particular situation and who is quiet. You wonder why. Perhaps you are able to place a particular student's work, attitude or demeanour in a larger context of classes throughout the year. You are quickly able to spot and assimilate any out-of-character behaviour.

So as a teacher in this scenario, you are constantly making a range of judgements based on your impressions of students working together, your conversations with them, your viewpoint about the quality of their design work and placing these judgements in a wider context or framework drawn from your knowledge of them and their work throughout the year. So how should you go about collecting and storing this type of assessment data? Where should you start? After all, there is so much useful data here that you could collect and use.

> **PRACTICAL TASK** PRACTICAL TASK PRACTICAL TASK PRACTICAL TASK PRACTICAL TASK
>
> Using the design and technology lesson described above as an example, write a short description of an episode from a lesson that you have observed recently that gave the teacher a good opportunity to gather a range of assessment data. Think about the different possibilities offered for assessment by the nature of the task, the students' engagement with the task or other aspects of the teaching and learning that you observed. If you get the opportunity, talk to the teacher about their planning for the lesson. Were any assessment opportunities or strategies identified beforehand? If so, did they materialise? If not, did other opportunities emerge as part of the natural flow of the lesson and where these were acted upon?

Firstly, it is important to remember that good assessment practice flows from good planning. Therefore, the focus for the collection of assessment data should relate to and be tied in with the stated learning objectives and associated learning outcomes for the lesson. While you should always be on the lookout for the unexpected, it is prudent to narrow your focus in situations like this and try to maintain a clear perspective on what it is that you are trying to find out about your students' learning through this particular task.

Secondly, you will need to be prepared to collect a range of data in this classroom scenario. Chief among these data will be records of students' conversations. Fragments of these could be noted down as you circulate. But unless you are an expert in shorthand, it is unlikely that you are going to be able to make anything more substantial than general notes about students' conversations. This may be fine. But what happens if an interesting conversation occurs that really makes you think hard about the task, the learning that is going on and the students' engagement with the learning environment you have constructed? In this case, perhaps an actual recording of the students' conversation might be valuable. Although you wouldn't want to have too many of these to listen back to, there is tremendous value in relistening to students' conversations at leisure and trying to make sense of their comments. In this case, the use of a portable recorder could be invaluable. Similarly, photographic evidence of students' work in progress and of them working can be a great stimulus for assessment. We naturally make judgements about the things that we see and visual cues or reminders can spur our thinking about a particular task and the students' response to it.

Thirdly, your time in the classroom is precious. Obtaining assessment data about your students' progress is only one of numerous roles that you will have to fulfil. With this in mind, it is important to try to establish a range of mechanisms for the collection of data. While you can be proactive in this role on occasions, it will be essential that you build in opportunities for students to create useful assessment data from their own learning processes. Processes by which students can self-evaluate their work, peer-appraise each other's work, or give feedback in other ways to members of their group will be particularly useful. All of these processes will provide you with more raw data which can be compiled and used at a later date.

Fourthly, you will need to develop a perceptive eye and ear for assessment. This is a skill and something that will develop with practice. While experienced teachers can plan for assessment opportunities in lessons, when you are beginning your teaching career this may be a little more haphazard. That said, it is very important to be attentive in your classroom. As a general rule, when students are working at something it is a good idea not to interrupt them too soon. Take time to listen to what they are saying, to watch what they are doing and try to make sense of their natural engagement with the various tasks or activities you have set them.

Finally from this scenario, remember that you will want to create a balance between the collection of summative assessment data (which you can keep and reflect on at a later date) and formative assessment data (which you can use also instantaneously to provide feedback to individuals or groups of students). Of course, that is not to say that one type of data is more valuable than the other. Fleeting, formative observations and comments may be particularly relevant and provide a useful backbone for more extensive, summative statements at a later date. The important thing is that all types of assessment data are collected and stored in such a way that you can begin the process of interpretation and analysis quickly and easily.

REFLECTIVE TASK

Think back on a lesson you have taught recently. Thinking about the points discussed above, briefly reflect on the following questions.

1. Did you plan for assessment opportunities in the lesson? Did they materialise?

2. What range of assessment data could you have collected, or did you collect, from the lesson?

3. How could you have, or did you, collect that evidence? Where did you put it?

4. Were you perceptive to the varying interactions between students, between students and the task/activities, or between yourself and the students during the lesson? Did you consciously take time to listen to and observe their learning in action?

5. How would you characterise the assessment data that you could have collected? Were they summative or formative in nature? What would have been most useful given the nature and/or content of the lesson?

Interpreting and analysing assessment data

Having collected a range of assessment data, it will be important to begin interpreting and analysing them as soon as possible after they have been collected. The longer the gap between the collection of the data and the process of interpretation and analysis, the more difficult it will be to treat the data in an authentic manner, i.e. in light of the context in which they were obtained. For that reason, we suggest that you try to make time for the interpretation and analysis of assessment data as a regular part of your teaching practice. This need not be a lengthy or laborious process. In many ways, it may be similar to processes of evaluation that you are asked to complete as part of your initial teacher training course. Like lesson evaluations, the interpretation and analysis of assessment data should have a twin focus and seek to identify a range of questions that relate to:

- **the consequences of your teaching and how this can be improved;**
- **what students have learnt and what evidence you have for their learning.**

In reality, the second of these two areas is likely to become the main focus of your interpretation and analysis as you move away from your period of initial teacher training into the first part of your teaching career. However, we maintain that students' learning is very closely linked to the teacher's pedagogy and that it is helpful to consider these two main elements together as you seek to obtain a clearer understanding of what students have learnt and how they have learnt it.

So what are the processes of interpretation and analysis that you are going to want to utilise? There are many different possibilities here. We present a few of the most common below to help you get started. However, it will be important that you conceptualise these in respect of your own subject area and try to find ways that work for you, in your particular teaching context and with your own particular groups of students.

Firstly, looking for general themes or common issues is a useful way of surveying large collections of textual or visual assessment data. You could ask a range of questions at this point.

- **What are the common issues or concerns that students are discussing in a particular lesson?**
- **Is it possible to categorise students' responses to a particular teaching task or activity?**
- **How have my students described the outcome of a particular teaching episode (perhaps through a plenary session)? Are there common responses that they have made? What are they?**

Secondly, it is often worth exploring key moments in lessons in more detail. You could try to identify what one might call 'key incidents' in your teaching. While describing these moments as 'eureka' moments might be a little dramatic, it is often possible to identify moments when things really seem to go well and students are totally engaged and clearly learning effectively. These special moments might be worthy of really rich and deep interpretation and analysis. In his book, *The Interpretation of Cultures*, Geertz (1973, pp5–6) calls this kind of approach 'thick description'. This phrase, adopted from the term originally described by the philosopher Gilbert Ryle, is illustrated by thinking about someone winking at you. If someone winks at you it could be for a whole range of reasons. It might be because the person is attracted to you, that they are trying to communicate secretly with you, that they understand what you mean, or something else. As the context changes, the meaning of the wink changes. Unless you have an understanding of the context, you won't know what the wink means. Geertz argues that all human behaviour is like this. He therefore distinguishes between what we might call 'thin description' (which, to extend our example, might just describe the wink itself) and a thick description (which explains the context of the wink and its wider implications).

Thick description is a helpful concept in light of our considerations of interpreting and analysing assessment data. It reminds us that such data are heavily contextualised within your classroom, the teaching that is being undertaken and the individual lives of your students. In today's climate with its penchant for number-crunched, statistical data it is helpful to remember that raw, contextualised data drawn from your own teaching often provide a much richer, fuller picture of students' learning 'in action'. These data are invaluable to you, not just as a means by which you can hone and refine your own teaching, but also as a way to gain insights into your students' learning.

Thirdly, you might want to conduct specific analyses of your data in response to particular questions or issues that you are facing in your teaching at a particular moment. Your course tutor or school-based mentor might generate these questions or issues or they may just be things that you would like to explore in more detail yourself. By way of an example, let's briefly consider the issue of how you might effectively cater for the needs of your gifted and talented students. (We will put to one side the issues of how these students might have been identified and assume that you know who these students are in a particular set of classes.)

In thinking about how your gifted and talented students are responding to your teaching, you might frame a simple research question to help you focus your analysis of the assessment data that you have collected. Using a simple research question like this could be conceptualised as a kind of lens through which you view your collected data with a particular kind of focus. It might prompt you to prioritise certain types of information or responses above others. You may even discard some of your collected data as being irrelevant for this particular focus. Perhaps you will need to go back to particular classes with this question in mind and collect a range of supplementary data. Either way, for a set period of time a set question or issue can become a defining and refining focus for your collection, interpretation and analysis of assessment data.

Fourthly, and finally, on occasions you will want to focus your interpretation and analysis of your assessment data on individual students. This might be for a range of reasons. Subject teachers are often asked to provide detailed accounts of individual students for individualised education plans or in response to requests by parents or others. Investigating an individual student's learning is sometimes not as easy as one might presume. It is important to remember that in our classrooms learning is socialised. It does not take place within the blank canvas of a student's mind and your instruction. It is mediated through resources, the classroom environment, other students, your pedagogy and previous learning experiences. Your interpretation and analysis of assessment data will need to take account of these defining contexts and try to present the richness of an individual student's learning against their backdrop. To do this, it will be essential that you can be perceptive to the richness of the classroom context within which learning has taken place, and from which you have recorded your assessment data.

PRACTICAL TASK PRACTICAL TASK PRACTICAL TASK PRACTICAL TASK PRACTICAL TASK

Having collected a range of assessment data from a lesson that you have taught, conduct a simple analysis of these data in one of the following ways.

1. Identify a range of general themes that have emerged from your data.
2. Use the concept of 'thick description' to write a short account of a particular moment in the lesson where ideas seemed to come particularly alive and meaningful for one student or a group of students.
3. Use the lenses of a 'framing' question to sift through your data and generate a simple analysis from them.
4. Take one student from your class and write about their learning in the lesson and how it related to the subject content, your pedagogy, the extended learning resources they engaged with, etc.

Finally, use your analysis to draw a range of implications for your own teaching and try to implement these evaluative findings in a forthcoming lesson of your choice.

Drawing conclusions from your assessment data

Finally in this first part of our consideration of the issues related to recording assessment data, we will turn to how you might draw conclusions from the assessment data that you have collected, interpreted and analysed. In some respects, the key issues have already been presented. So this section will be a brief summary of key themes from this chapter so far.

Firstly, all assessment data that you collect are embedded or contextualised within your teaching. As such, they need to be treated with care. The drawing of conclusions from the data will, in nearly every case, be tentative and not easily generalisable to other teachers or classrooms. This is a strength not a weakness (whatever others might say). It reinforces your essential professional role and identity in relation to the teaching that you have undertaken and the students' learning that you have observed and begun to understand. Obtaining, developing and describing this rich account of student learning based on assessment data is a key function of your role as a teacher. It's not just about raw scores to simple (or complex) tests and statistical analysis. It's about the complicated and interesting worlds that real students inhabit, the confusing and often messy learning pathways that they construct and the privileged positions that we, as teachers, have in working alongside them within our subject areas. Minimising or disempowering assessment to standardised tests or simple summative statistical devices doesn't help anyone, least of all you.

Having said that, you will be required to draw conclusions from your assessment data for a range of audiences. These will include senior school managers and, at least on a yearly basis, for parents via reporting mechanisms. At this point it will be essential that you are able to create simple descriptions of individual students' learning from your data and be able to justify these, should you be required to, at a later date. It is always useful to illustrate the bare facts of what an individual student has achieved in a particular year with descriptions of their work (either in progress or the finished products) from your classroom observations.

But perhaps the most important personal application of your work in drawing conclusions from your assessment data will be to inform your own teaching. This is something that you will become familiar with in your initial teacher training year. Good processes of recording assessment will not only provide you with a clear insight in what your students have learnt and how they have learnt it, they will also provide you with a mirror through which you can reflect on your teaching and its effectiveness.

Tools to help in recording assessment

Recording assessment in the ways described above may seem like an awful lot of work. Perhaps you are wondering how it can be achieved. We suggest that it has to become a manageable process and one that has to be accommodated alongside your many other roles as a teacher. Elements of recording assessment in this way may seem laborious, but we believe that it is very worthwhile. And as we will see below, there are all kinds of tools out there to help you record assessment quickly and easily. Some of these will have been designed for this purpose; others will need to be skilfully adapted. Either way, there is a range of tried-and-trusted methods that we'd like to discuss briefly, as well as some new approaches that we believe will be very helpful.

This section will be divided into three main parts. The first will discuss tools that will help you collect assessment data; the second will consider tools that will help you store, manage and investigate the data; the third will identify some tools that will help you present assessment data.

Tools that assist the collection of assessment data

There is nothing like a simple pencil and paper for the collection of assessment data. It's straightforward and immediate. The only things that can go wrong are broken leads and a lack of space. We'll be considering the role of teachers' mark books below.

Simple numerical or text data could also be collected through digital devices such as PDAs or certain mobile phones. Many of these allow you to run basic versions of word processing, spreadsheet or database programs that can then by synced to your computer, allowing the data to be transferred automatically.

But what about all that other type of data that you might want to collect in support of your assessment practices? There is a range of simple technologies that can help you collect assessment data. Perhaps the most common and useful are digital cameras, digital audio recorders and digital video cameras.

Digital cameras are simple to operate and, for the purposes of collecting photographic evidence in classrooms, relatively cheap and easy to use. Many mobile phones have high-quality cameras built in. Even those with minimal photographic skills can take simple, high-quality photographs of students working together on the various pieces of work that they might produce in a lesson. Most digital cameras will connect to a computer through USB and there are numerous free pieces of software that will help you organise and store collections of photographs.

Digital audio recorders have developed significantly in recent years. Although Minidisc recorders used to be very popular, we would suggest that the new range of hard-disk recorders are worth exploring for the purposes of classroom use. While it is beyond the scope of this chapter to give a detailed analysis of any particular product, we will talk about some general characteristics of products currently available from technology suppliers.

The majority of new digital audio recorders are highly portable, often not being larger than a standard MP3 player. They have built-in, high-quality condenser microphones and allow you to record directly onto an SD card. This is tremendously helpful as it means that you won't need to worry about attaching an external microphone. Many of these recorders are very easy to use. You just press 'Record', adjust your recording level, press Record again and you get a fantastic quality recording from the built-in stereo microphones. Every detail is captured and recorded directly onto the SD card. Transferring the recording to a computer is also simple via the supplied USB cable. Simple editing functions can also be accomplished with ease via intuitive interfaces.

As with any type of recording, there is a certain amount of technique that needs to be learnt. You will want to consider how to position the recording device in relation to the sound being recorded, select the right recording options, etc. But these decisions are made very easy through intuitive interfaces and the simple switches on these highly portable recorders.

The use of digital video cameras can also be very useful for those subjects that have a performance dimension to their work. Digital video can be captured and transferred to a computer through USB 2.0 or Firewire connectivity. Digital video files are significantly larger in size than digital audio and, in order to avoid spending excessive time transferring files, you'll want to make sure that any video recordings that you take are selected carefully and focused. Even the process of editing video recordings can be very time consuming. There will be more on this below.

Finally, mobile phones increasingly contain many of the functions of these other pieces of technology. They can certainly be used to collect photographs and short snippets of videos. The synchronisation of phones to computers has improved considerably in recent years. If you work in a school with a more liberal policy about students' uses of mobile phones within the classroom then you could certainly get students involved in the collection of a range of data of this type.

PRACTICAL TASK PRACTICAL TASK PRACTICAL TASK PRACTICAL TASK PRACTICAL TASK

Try to obtain one of the pieces of technology described above. Play with it until you are happy about how to use it confidently. Take it into a lesson that you are teaching and use it to collect some assessment data. If appropriate, why not ask a student to help you at some point in the collection of some of these data?

Tools that assist the storage, management and investigation of assessment data

Whatever type of assessment data you are recording, you'll need to have a well-organised system for their storage and management. We'll be considering three approaches below: firstly, the traditional teacher's mark book; secondly, the use of a range of generic software; and finally specific assessment software tools.

The traditional mark book

Teachers' mark books have a long, tried-and-tested history. They can contain a huge range of material and information, organised in classes, that have the potential to be a tremendous help to you in recording assessment data. By their nature, they facilitate the recording of numerical or, on occasions, textual information. But teachers have a range of personal codes or marks that they use to help record information. There are too many of these to go into in a lot of detail here. As part of your initial teacher training experience you should ask to look at a number of different teachers' mark books and investigate the different kinds of shorthand that they adopt within them. For example, one common way to indicate a student's progression through a particular task is via the use of a triangle; one side means working towards, two sides are working at, and the full triangle is working beyond. Figure 9.1 shows an example of this.

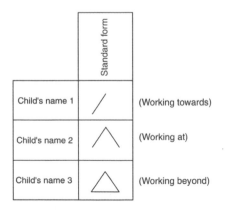

Figure 9.1 Example mark book extract

Other systems can be found which are equally appropriate and informative. These needn't be complicated. A simple red dot next to a student's name when they answer a question correctly can soon build up an interesting pattern that shows which students are responding well to your teaching.

Generic software tools

There is a range of software tools that will be useful in the management and storage of assessment data. Organisational software such as *iTunes* or *Windows Media Player*, *iPhoto* or *Picasa* and *iMovie* or *Windows Movie Maker* can be very helpful in managing collections of audio, photographic or video material. Or something as simple as a well-organised folder structure within your PC can create a more personalised space for storage, as in the example in Figure 9.2.

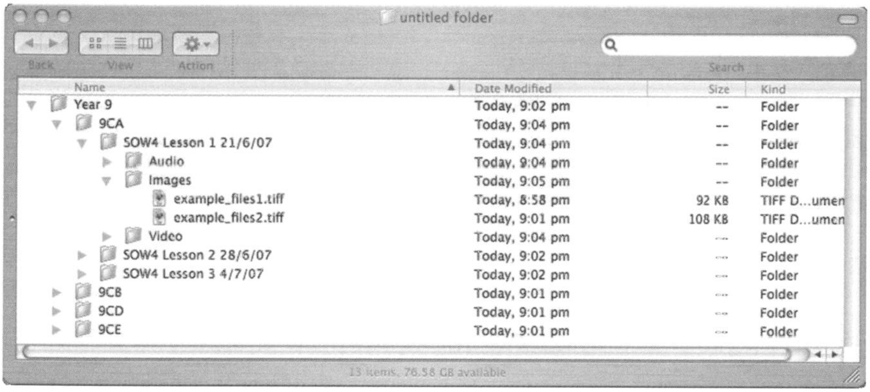

Figure 9.2 An organised folder structure

Either way, it is useful to consider the use of specific file names for collections of digital files. All the devices discussed above tend to save digital files with abstract or numerical file names, e.g. 100-0013.tiff. Lists of these can become very disorientating and unhelpful, as illustrated in Figure 9.3.

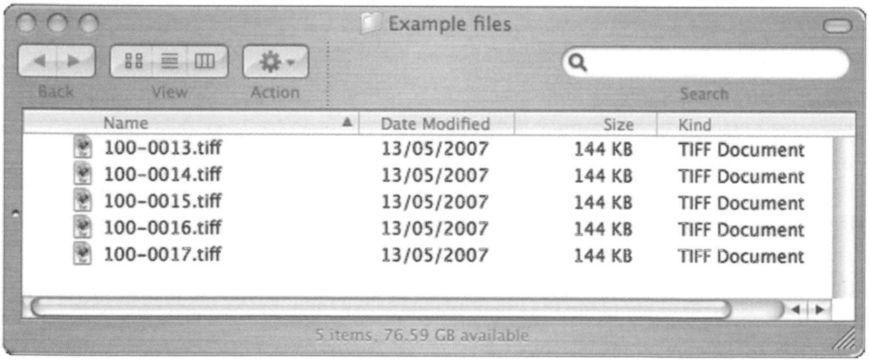

Figure 9.3 Disorientating file names

It is important to name your files in such a way that the names will help you remember when and perhaps where you recorded them. (See Figure 9.4.) There is a range of freeware pieces of software that allow you to create multiple personalised file names for folders of digital files. On Macintosh computers you can use a pre-programmed Automator script to do this.

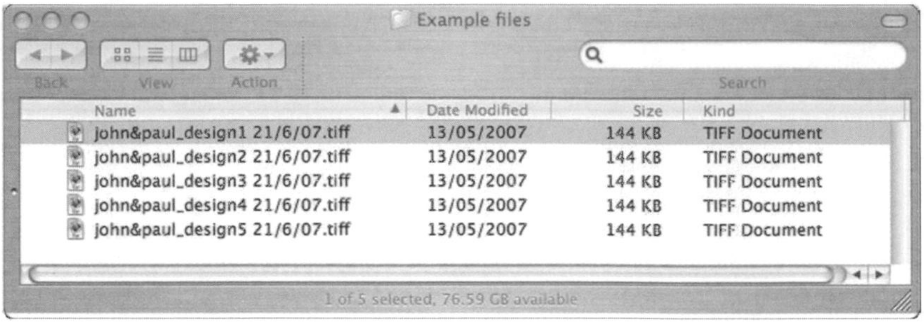

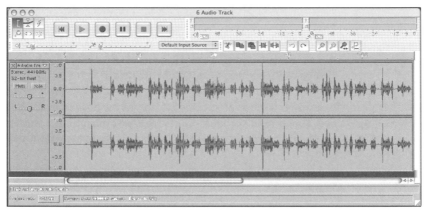

Figure 9.4 Informing file names

Careful editing of digital files is also important and need not be too time consuming. There is a range of potential tools to help you here. Many of these come bundled free with *Windows Vista* or *XP* and Apple computers have a tremendous range of free software too. Software such *iPhoto* or *Picasa*, *iMovie* and *Windows Movie Maker* allow you to edit photographic and video files simply. For audio files, the free software *Audacity* is available for PC and Mac computers. It is a simple audio editor that also allows you to save files in .wav or .mp3 format. As you can see in Figure 9.5, the interface is simple and not too threatening. It is an ideal way to quickly edit files that you might have recorded on a portable recorder such as the Edirol R-09.

Figure 9.5 *Audacity*'s main window

In addition to these multimedia tools, traditional software tools such as word processors, spreadsheets and databases can all play an important role in helping you store and manage assessment data. Spreadsheets can become a kind of twenty-first-century mark book and automate a range of functions that will be particularly useful with numerical or text data. Make sure that you obtain a basic knowledge of how to create simple spreadsheet formulas such as SUM, ADD, AVERAGE, COUNT IF, etc. These will become invaluable if you collect a lot of numerical or text-based data.

Within suites of software, such as *Microsoft Office* or *NeoOffice*, why not think about making use of the linking functions between files or data via html? It is very simple to code particular words or phrases and create links to other data stored on your computer. This can save you a lot of time when you are busy searching for information or wanting to move between particular files while looking for evidence.

Finally, the intelligent search functions on modern computers can assist you in finding data. Like any tool, it is important to learn how to use it constructively and create comprehensive search strings that locate the precise information that you are looking for. Also, remember that search tools such as Apple's Spotlight search within file content as well as file names and are particularly powerful.

Specific software tools

Increasingly, many schools are buying dedicated assessment software to help teachers manage the process of recording assessment. These assessment tools can be very helpful and very powerful. Networked tools such as *eSAAMS* allow schools to create individual student record cards with basic information and a photograph. Students are grouped into classes and registration details and seating plans can be arranged within the software. Audio and video files of their work in progress or finished products can be captured and stored within the software and you can also mark the work using a tailor-made marking scheme of your own design. Different subject areas can produce their own variations on marking schemes. The software manages each student's individual assessment history and data can be exported out of *eSAAMS* into other database software for more detailed analysis.

Tools such as *eSAAMS* are not cheap but they do offer good functionality and assist the busy classroom teacher. While undergoing initial teacher training, you will probably not be working in a school that makes use of such a piece of software. But many of the skills and processes that we have described above can be done with a modestly equipped PC and a few external pieces of hardware such as a mobile phone, camera or recorder. We think it is important that you work through the issues associated with these pieces of hardware and software. By doing so you will create a personalised system for the collection, storage and management of your recorded assessment data. This will greatly facilitate your general day-to-day teaching.

PRACTICAL TASK PRACTICAL TASK PRACTICAL TASK PRACTICAL TASK PRACTICAL TASK

Take some time to talk with other teachers in your school about how they store and manage assessment data. Make some notes about the range of methods, paper-based or electronic, that they use. Are there any whole-school approaches that you notice? If so, talk to the assessment co-ordinator about why they chose that particular piece of software or method. What are the perceived advantages? How has it been received by staff? What are its facilitating dimensions? Are there any drawbacks?

Tools that assist the presentation of assessment data

Finally, a chapter on recording assessment data would not be complete without a brief consideration of some of the issues associated with presenting assessment data. In recent years there has been an explosion in the creation of electronic portfolio systems that allow users to organise and present electronic content. These take a number of shapes and forms that are too numerous to present a complete account of here. Rather, we will briefly consider two fairly well-known applications that contain elements of ePortfolio systems.

It is hard to find a precise definition for an electronic portfolio, as the terminology is quite hotly debated amongst practitioners. This definition from a Wikipedia page is a good starting point:

> *An electronic portfolio is a collection of electronic evidence (artefacts, including inputted text, electronic files such as Word and PDF files, images, multimedia, blog entries and Web links, etc) assembled and managed by a user, usually online. ePortfolios are both demonstrations of the user's abilities and platforms for self-expression, and, if they are online, they can be maintained dynamically over time. Some ePortfolio applications permit varying degrees of audience access, so the same portfolio might be used for multiple purposes.*
>
> **(http://en.wikipedia.org/wiki/Electronic_Portfolio**; accessed 14/6/07)

ePortfolios present a new level of sophistication in the presentation of assessment data. In many ways they can assist the teacher in allowing the student a greater degree of access and control over the presentation of their work to an intended audience. This can be achieved very simply with students of all ages, certainly in Key Stage 2 upwards. Many educational courseware solutions such as Moodle (**www.moodle.org**) contain elements of ePortfolio design and integration. Other related examples, such as Elgg (**www.elgg.org**), provide users with their own weblog, file repository, online profile and RSS reader. While this is similar to other social networking sites such as MySpace, with Elgg users can give certain degrees of control over who can access their content. This would be particularly useful in a teaching context where you might want to limit access to a student's work. In contrast to Moodle, which is really a sophisticated virtual learning environment with powerful assessment tools built in for teachers to use, an environment such as Elgg provides a more informal space that lets students exercise their own thoughts and reflections and make their own connections between content. They can compile their own body of evidence, akin to a traditional ePortfolio, and invite others to interact with this evidence.

Conclusion

ePortfolios represent one way ahead for the presentation of assessment data. They can place a significant degree of ownership and control in the hands of the student. Some may see this as problematic. Others see it as an opportunity to personalise the recording of assessment data and truly empower students with a skill set fit for the twenty-first century. You'll have to decide!

A SUMMARY OF **KEY POINTS**

> There is a range of assessment data 'types' that you will want to collect, store and analyse.
> Recording assessment begins with the collection and storing of data. Being perceptive to the learning that is going on in your classroom is a prerequisite of good assessment practice.
> Interpreting and analysing data can be done in a number of ways. Whatever way you choose, make sure that you do it as soon after the lesson as possible while it is fresh in your mind.
> Drawing conclusions from your assessment data is important, but remember that these are contextualised in your teaching and that this is their strength not their weakness.
> There are various tools out there to help you in the process of recording assessment. Make use of a range of technologies to help you collect, store and investigate your assessment data.
> Beware of assessment data overload. Be selective and make sure that the teaching/assessment horse and cart are the right way around.

REFERENCES REFERENCES **REFERENCES** REFERENCES **REFERENCES** REFERENCES

Geertz, C. (1973) *The interpretation of cultures*. New York: Basic Books.

FURTHER READING FURTHER READING **FURTHER READING** FURTHER READING

Black, P., Harrison, C., Lee, C., Marshall, B. and Wiliam, D. (2003) *Assessment for learning: putting it into practice*. Maidenhead: Open University Press/McGraw-Hill Education.

Brooks, V. (2002) *Assessment in secondary schools: The new teacher's guide to monitoring, assessment, recording, reporting and accountability*. Maidenhead: Open University Press/McGraw-Hill Education.

Clarke, S. (2005) *Formative assessment in the secondary classroom*. London: Hodder Murray.

10
Your future development

Chapter objectives

By the end of this chapter you should have:

- **begun to put together the various strands from this book to think about how you can use assessment in the classroom;**
- **understood that ideas relating to assessment need not remain static;**
- **developed purposeful strategies that will lead towards reflective practice as an important aspect to your development as a teacher;**
- **analysed 'reflection-in-action' and 'reflection-on-action' as keys to understanding the links between teaching, learning and assessment;**
- **built on, and developed, the practical task from Chapter 1 into a personalised needs analysis;**
- **developed strategies that focus on your students as a source for reflective action and for the formation of personal targets in the area of assessment.**

Professional Standards for QTS

This chapter will help you to meet the following Professional Standards for QTS: Q7ab, Q8, Q9, Q12, Q14, Q22, Q26ab, Q27, Q28, Q29, Q32

Introduction

Throughout this book we have considered the ways in which you can develop your assessment practices when working with students in schools. We have provided you with ideas, suggested things to try out, given you things to think about, challenged your preconceptions, and offered you provocations upon which to reflect. We have done this at an early point in your teaching career and, we trust, inspired you really to think about assessment from the outset. We now turn to what you will need to do in the coming months and years as you move from being a trainee teacher, through your NQT year and beyond into your teaching career. In the opening section of Chapter 1 we made the observation that good assessment practice is a key feature of effective teaching and learning in schools. Your task now is to bring the words of this book alive off the page in your lessons, and make good assessment practice a day-to-day reality in your classroom.

One of this book's resounding themes has focused on the integration of assessment within teaching and learning. As a subset of this, we have also emphasised the importance of a student-centred approach to assessment and prioritised formative assessment (as an umbrella term covering a range of practices and ideas) as a way to develop your teaching, and promote your students' learning, most effectively.

In this final chapter we turn the focus back on you and where you are going to go from here. Your initial teacher training year is full of various stresses and strains. You will have faced many challenges and, we trust, will have conquered many of them. We are sure that you will have learnt many new things and feel well equipped to face your NQT year. But learning to teach is a lifelong process and the stages of development that you will go through will each feel quite distinct and different. This is difficult to describe but is illustrated well by the transition point that you have reached. The NQT year is very different in tone from your training year. You will be a full member of the academic staff of a school and this changes significantly the way in which students treat you. Hopefully you will encounter a greater degree of respect from students and find that your authority is enhanced. Although you will have a designated mentor to assist you throughout this year and complete the Career Entry Development Profile (CEDP), in many ways you will be left to get on with your teaching day by day. This is often a great feeling and one that you will enjoy. After all, it is what you have been prepared for.

Evaluating teaching and learning

Learning to teach is a lifelong process because teaching and learning are complex, dynamic and interactive processes that occur between individuals, individuals and particular institutions, and individuals and various resources and materials. These processes occur in real time, in an 'instant' which cannot easily be repeated. While you may come to hold a clear theoretical view of what these processes entail, it is also important to recognise the views that others hold, not least your students, and that theoretical understandings can be challenged through practice. Bruner's notion of 'folk pedagogy' reinforces this point, emphasising the importance of understanding the potential conflicts that can erupt within a learning environment like a classroom if one is insensitive as a teacher to students' views of education:

> You had better take into account the folk theories that those engaged in teaching and learning already have. For any innovations that you, as a 'proper' pedagogical theorist, may wish to introduce will have to compete with, replace, or otherwise modify the folk theories that already guide both teachers and students.
>
> (Bruner, 1996, p46)

It is clear that learning to teach is a gradual process that centres on the adoption of a complicated set of skills that will, at a basic level, develop over time. Furlong and Maynard (1995) have conceptualised the development of trainee teachers in the following five stages.

1. Early idealism: clear, if idealistic, views as to what sort of teachers they wanted to be.
2. Personal survival: idealism fades when confronted with classroom realities, and 'fitting in' becomes most important, especially with regard to behaviour management.
3. Dealing with difficulties: trainees begin to make sense of things, and achieve a measure of classroom control.
4. Hitting a plateau: having found a way of teaching which 'works', more or less, a trainee sticks with it, and does not deviate from it.
5. Moving on: trainees worked with tutors, supervisors and mentors, to understand that there was a need to change.

As you progress through your training you are likely to find yourself moving through these stages, and will need to develop your own ways of dealing with them.

Becoming a reflective practitioner

Thoughout this book we have emphasised the importance of planning for learning. Continuing this theme, one of the most important ways in which you can develop yourself as a teacher is to be found in a section which often figures towards the end of your planning documentation; this is the lesson evaluation section. Writing lesson evaluations, as we discussed in Chapter 6, might seem a chore at times, but not only do they offer a useful source of evidence for planning for your next lesson, they also allow you, over time, to build up reflections which really allow you to take learning forwards. Chapter 9 offered suggestions for some innovative ways in which you could record assessment data. It will be up to you to make use of this in developing your professional practice. There is a saying to the effect that 'some teachers have ten years' experience of teaching, others have one year's experience which they have repeated ten times!'. You will want to be in the former category, we hope. One way of starting on this road is to revisit your lesson evaluations, and see what it is that they are able to tell you over time, as well as in the immediate aftermath of a lesson. So don't just write them and file them, interrogate them for what they are telling you – or maybe not telling you – about developing assessment practices over time.

What you will be doing by undertaking this review of your evaluations is taking early steps along the road to becoming a reflective practitioner. Schön (1983) described what takes place during reflection. He suggested that this happens in two ways; these are reflection-in-action and reflection-on-action. Reflection-in-action is what takes place when you reflect on what you are doing as you are doing it, whereas reflection-on-action is reflection which you undertake once the event has taken place. The written lesson evaluations we have been discussing are likely to take the form of reflection-on-action, as you will be writing these once the lesson is over. Reflection-in-action will develop, but it is possible that it will take a little time to develop. It is the capacity to engage in reflection-in-action that is one of the distinguishing characteristics of an experienced teacher. This allows the practitioner to reshape and redirect the lesson as it takes place, and to maximise the learning potential of their students accordingly.

PRACTICAL TASK PRACTICAL TASK PRACTICAL TASK PRACTICAL TASK PRACTICAL TASK

One of the ways in which you can develop your capacity for reflection-in-action is to be found in your lesson planning documentation. Many planning pro-formas allow you to plan for activities with timings. This means you can plan, say, seven minutes for a starter activity, six minutes for the next part of the lesson, and so on. You may find, like many beginning teachers, that in your early lessons you overrun, as you are following the sequence of activities but finding they take much longer than you thought. In many cases this is because as a beginning teacher you follow your lesson plans in a linear fashion from beginning to end. What you will find more experienced colleagues in schools doing is to 'on-the-hoof' mentally plan backwards from the end-time of the lesson. They know how much time is left, and then undertake reflection-in-action to work out the most efficacious way of sequencing the lesson to fit it into the available time remaining. As you get more experienced in the classroom try this reflection-in-action way of working yourself, and then reflect-on-action as to what sort of difference it made to your lesson delivery.

Evaluative shift from teaching to learning

As a beginning teacher, it is almost inevitable that your early lesson evaluations will focus on teaching. After all, what you will be doing is often called 'teaching practice', and one aspect of being on teaching practice is the opportunity to practise your teaching. In other words, you can rehearse your teaching, and try things out in the classroom. However, as time progresses you, and your tutors, supervisors and mentors, will become more concerned with your evaluations focusing upon your students' *learning* and the ways that you can encourage this through a range of appropriate assessment strategies. Figure 10.1 demonstrates how your focus should shift over time, from a focus on teaching, to a focus on learning.

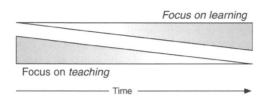

Figure 10.1 Shifting focus from teaching to learning

The change Figure 10.1 shows is an important shift in your perception, and marks another factor in your emergence as a reflective practitioner.

Assessment as an engine of change

The engine that will drive this shift, evidenced in your reflections, is formative assessment. To add weight to the formative assessment observations you have made, summative assessment data will also prove to be useful. In developing your practice with regard to assessment you will also be concerned with reflecting on the assessment processes and the products of assessment, i.e. the data you have collected, the formative assessment comments you made, and the feedback you gave. The evaluations you make of your lessons are another form of assessment data, and may well include formative assessment information on both you and the students you are teaching.

Engaging in a period of reflection after you have undertaken a piece of assessment should focus on aspects that you can influence on future occasions, and on how to deal with those over which you only have limited control. If the focus of your reflection has been on the assessment process, then consider what aspects of the doing of the task went well, and try to account for why this was. It is human nature that you will also want to consider what did not go quite so well. Again ask yourself why, and, critically, what you could do about it next time you undertake this sort of activity. If your focus was on assessment product then questions to ask yourself include the appropriateness of the assessment used, and whether the data it yields are valuable, reliable and fit for purpose.

Practical task for your future development

As part of Chapter 1, we asked you to consider some fundamental questions about the purposes and practices of assessment. In that practical task, you were presented with a range of provocative statements aimed at helping you to summarise your current understanding of assessment at that point.

Since then, we hope that you have read the chapters that followed carefully and worked methodically through the various practical and reflective tasks. Having done this, you will have constructed a significant amount of information about your own assessment practice and, we hope, about how this can be developed and improved. You will have obtained new insights into your own developing teaching practice and drawn on the experiences of other teachers to support your work at that crucial stage in your development.

As part of this transition from beginning teacher to NQT, it will be important for you to prioritise key elements of your teaching practice for further development. The CEDP process we mentioned earlier is designed to assist this in a general way and is built around a number of transition points. The first of these is managed by your initial teacher education provider; the second and third by your new school. As part of this process, you will be asked to set targets for your NQT year, identify resources that will help you meet these targets, and then reflect on your progress against these targets.

To assist your future development in the area of assessment, we have designed a simple practical task that will act as a conclusion to this book. It follows a similar process to that adopted by the CEDP (and may, indeed, help you in the completion of that important document) but builds on the main themes of this book. It is devised in four main parts.

Firstly, the task asks you to reconsider each of the eight key questions identified in Chapter 1. These 'Key assessment questions' are then followed by 'Key developmental questions' that relate to the main structure of the book. Here, you will find questions that probe your understanding of the book's main themes, including summative assessment, formative assessment, student-centred assessment strategies, planning for assessment opportunities, differentiation, uses of ICT and much more.

Secondly, in response to each of the Key assessment questions and the associated Key developmental questions we have asked you to identify a range of targets for your own professional development. Target setting is a common process in education nowadays and is an important part of most performance management strategies that you will find in school. When setting targets for your own performance, the SMART acronym is a useful starting point for your consideration.

S	*Specific*	They say exactly what you mean.
M	*Measurable*	You can prove that you have reached them.
A	*Achievable*	You can reach them in the identified time period.
R	*Realistic*	They are about action you can take.
T	*Time-related*	They have deadlines that are realistic.

There is also a range of other resources available to help you with the target-setting process. The DfES website contains a range of helpful information about the target-setting process which you may find useful (DfES, 2007).

Thirdly, with each target that you set for your personal development in this area, we suggest that you identify any resources that you might need to help you fulfil it. Resources might include:

- **additional information (see the Further reading identified at the end of each chapter within this book as a good starting point for this);**

- time to observe other teachers who are working through similar issues in their teaching or who may be more experienced than you;
- access to particular resources (including ICT) that will help support your developing assessment practices.

Fourthly, it is vital that you put a clear and realistic timeline in place for your targets. The target-setting process will end with a period of review and evaluation where, at its most mundane, you will determine whether or not you have met the target. More helpfully, this part of the process should help you identify areas for future developments in your teaching practice.

With these thoughts in mind, we suggest that you work through the practical task on pages 133–6 with an eye on your future teaching practice. If you know where you are going to be teaching in your NQT year, you could share this planning process with your new mentor and write targets that relate to the classes that you are going to teach. If not, the general focus of the questions will still help you plan appropriately for the next stage of your teaching development.

In undertaking this practical task you will have produced a needs analysis for your future development which you can share with your NQT mentors as part of the CEDP process, and as an ongoing part of your future professional development.

PRACTICAL TASK PRACTICAL TASK **PRACTICAL TASK** PRACTICAL TASK **PRACTICAL TASK**

Some of the initial statements in the practical task are deliberately quite provocative. As you have worked through this book, and gained more experience in schools, have your opinions to any of these provocations changed?

Part of developing into a reflective practitioner is being open to change, and to be able to form and reform your opinions, so if you have changed your mind, this is no bad thing. Sometimes as you progress through your career and reflect on issues you will realise that things you once believed may no longer be the case. Indeed, this is one way in which you can avoid having the same year's experience ten times over.

The way forwards

We have emphasised many times in this book that the important aspect of assessment is that it should be used to improve learning, not just measure it. This aspect of assessment practice cannot be overstated. Despite a proliferation of ring-binders and other support materials, there are worries that many teachers working in schools for a number of years have been forced into assessment regimes which may not be helpful to the development of their subjects. The development of testing for atomistic pieces of knowledge in order to improve test scores can mask a paucity of understanding of deeper and wider issues of subject knowledge amongst students. After all:

. . . the clearer you are about what you want, the more likely you are to get it – but the less likely it is to mean anything.

(Wiliam, 2001, p60)

Or, as Wiliam notes elsewhere in the same article:

We start out with the aim of making the important measurable and end up making only the measurable important.

(Wiliam, 2001, p58)

This is an easy trap to fall into, and the current insistence on 'levelling' in National Curriculum terms has an unfortunate side-effect linguistically, as 'levelling' also means to bring everything to the same level. Using National Curriculum assessment information is obviously an important part of your job, but, as we discussed in Chapter 6, using summative assessment information in a formative fashion is not the only way in which you should be thinking about formative assessment.

> ### CLASSROOM STORY
> A PGCE student on teaching practice was told by the school's assessment manager that assessment for learning consisted of giving the students a National Curriculum level as frequently as possible, and building these up over time to be able to give 'accurate' level information on reports. The student was concerned, as that did not tally with her understanding from reading and professional studies sessions. Her subject mentor in school shared her concerns.

The way of looking at assessment in the classroom story above shows a way of thinking about formative assessment which reduces it to a series of mini-summative assessments. The beginning teacher found this unhelpful, as she wanted to engage in formative assessment strategies at a higher level, including many of the techniques we discussed in Chapter 4, but felt unable to, owing to the school's approach. The moral of this story is that interpretations of assessment and, it seems particularly of formative assessment, are not fixed, and that you might find that people are using the terminologies in ways which you do not recognise. The ongoing and formative use of summative assessment is, of course, entirely possible, as we saw in Chapter 5. However, this approach is likely to miss out all the finer points of the proper use of formative assessment. When the beginning teacher reported back to her general mentor in school, discussions with the assessment manager were established, and the benefit of the beginning teacher's recent and relevant experience were valued by the school. So a second moral of this story is that, if you have concerns, raise them with someone; just because you are inexperienced does not mean you are automatically wrong.

Once you are established in post, then you will be able to formulate your own systems for working, and establish your own classroom routines. In Chapter 3 we discussed the use of peer- and self-assessment techniques. In post you have a greater opportunity to establish practices such as this to be a normal part of your ongoing classroom work. Developing and maintaining strategies like this over time will enable your students to become more engaged in the processes of their own learning. Doing this will involve you in another form of reflection, where you reflect on actions that you have undertaken in your classroom, and it is to this notion of inquiry-for-reflection that we now turn.

Action research as reflection

It is quite possible that you have had to undertake a small research project as part of your ITT, maybe a small-scale case study, or an action research project. Both of these forms of enquiry will have involved you in thinking about, and reflecting on, aspects of educational provision that you have observed. In the case of action research the methodology that is usually employed has direct transferability to the way we are advising you to reflect on aspects of your own educational situation in your classroom. ✍

RESEARCH SUMMARY RESEARCH SUMMARY **RESEARCH SUMMARY** RESEARCH SUMMARY

The origins of the notion of action research are not altogether clear, but it is known that the German Psychologist Kurt Lewin, who during the 1940s was working in America, was discussing how undertaking action research was 'proceeding in a spiral of steps, each of which is composed of planning, action and the evaluation of the result of action' (Kemmis and McTaggart, 1990, p8).

This essential feature of action research, the notion of a spiral consisting of four stages (Figure 10.2) is highly appropriate for you to use as the basis for your reflections on the work that you and your students do with regard to assessment in the classroom.

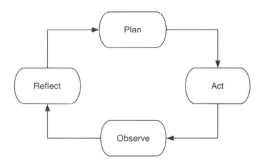

Figure 10.2 Action research spiral

The four stages of action research identified in Figure 10.2 are as follows.

- **Plan:** Here you plan for the assessment strategy (or strategies) which you will be employing.
- **Act:** In this phase the assessments you have planned are implemented.
- **Observe:** While the implementation is taking place, you observe and note what is going on, undertake assessments, give feedback, and evaluate actions and processes as they happen, and undertake reflection in action as much as possible.
- **Reflect:** In this stage you look back on what happened and engage in reflection on action.

The notion of action research operating in a spiral means that from the first occurrence there is a link to subsequent iterations, building up into a spiral over time. Each subsequent 'rotation' builds on knowledge acquired from previous occasions.

Using the action research spiral as a model for reflection and evaluation serves a number of functions. It enables you to undertake structured reflection on assessment work done by you and the students in your classes, and it enables you to learn from what you have done in order to do things differently in subsequent occasions. Using this model also enables you to tailor your work to different classes' responses. Although intended as a research methodology, using this way of inquiry-for-reflection in your own classroom will provide you with some very powerful and rich data that you will be able to draw on for your future development. Indeed, this can be considered as an instance of self-assessment in which you personally engage, a sort of meta-assessment where you endeavour to evaluate the approaches which you have adopted in your classroom.

Using the action research as a model is also a suitable route for another aspect of your future development, this being higher-level studies in education, possibly in the form of a masters degree, such as an MA or an MEd. Setting up classroom projects which utilise action research methodologies is a common component of many university in-service degrees for teachers. It also forms the basis for many self-help initiatives which local authorities organise for their teachers.

Conclusion

Making and using your own judgements is, as we have seen, a key aspect of formative assessment. As a beginning teacher you will have been developing your pedagogical content knowledge, and will continue to do so throughout your career. Your own evaluative judgements are a key part of this, and it is upon application of your judgements that the future direction of the learning of your classes will depend.

A SUMMARY OF **KEY POINTS**

> **Learning to teach is a lifelong process with many distinct and different stages of development.**

> **Careful planning and evaluation of your teaching will help you to become a reflective practitioner as you gain experience.**

> **A reflective practitioner is open to change, forming and re-forming opinions.**

> **Assessment should be used to improve learning, not simply to measure it.**

REFERENCES REFERENCES **REFERENCES** REFERENCES **REFERENCES** REFERENCES

Bruner, J. (1996) *The culture of education.* Cambridge, Mass.: Harvard University Press.

DfES (2007) *Target setting.* **www.standards.dfes.gov.uk/ts/** (accessed 27 June 2007)

Furlong, J. and Maynard, T. (1995) *Mentoring student teachers – the growth of professional knowledge.* London: Routledge.

Kemmis, S.E. and McTaggart, R.E. (1990) *The action research planner.* Victoria, Australia: Deakin University.

Schön, D. (1983) *The reflective practitioner.* Aldershot: Academic Publishing.

Wiliam, D. (2001) What is wrong with our educational assessment and what can be done about it? *Education Review,* 15(1): 57–62.

PRACTICAL TASK PRACTICAL TASK PRACTICAL TASK PRACTICAL TASK PRACTICAL TASK

Planning your future assessment practices

Key assessment questions (from Chapter 1)	Key developmental questions	Key developmental targets	Resources needed	Review/ Evaluation
Why do we assess?	Having read this book, how can I define the main purpose of assessment in my subject?			
	What further reading or study do I need to undertake to develop my knowledge of why assessment is important in education?			
What is assessment?	How can I extend the range of summative and formative assessment types in my teaching?			
	Is there a correct balance between the various assessment types for the teaching in my subject? How will I know when I have achieved this?			
	What are the problems associated with an overemphasis on one particular form of assessment? How can these be mitigated?			
	Where can I go to develop my knowledge and obtain further information about the range and appropriateness of different assessment types for the teaching of my subject?			

What is your role?

As my teaching develops during the early part of my career, what checks and balances can I adopt to ensure that my assessment practice remains integrated within my teaching?

In particular, how can I develop my assessment practice in the following key areas over the next year?

1. Effective planning for assessment.
2. Sharing learning objectives and assessment criteria with students.
3. Ensuring that a full range of knowledge is defined, presented and assessed.
4. Planning for assessment conversations with students.
5. Developing a range of approaches for questioning students about their learning.
6. Differentiating tasks for progression.
7. Providing constructive feedback and feed forward to students.
8. Marking and grading students' work constructively.
9. Rewarding effort and achievement.

What is the role of the student – individually – collectively?		
	What changes in my teaching practice do I need to make to place the student at the heart of assessment in my classroom?	
	If 'assessment as enquiry' is my chosen paradigm for assessment in my teaching, how can I ensure that this sense of shared or collaborative enquiry is sustained lesson by lesson, between units of work and across the key stages?	
	How can I increase the range of student-centred assessment processes in my teaching? In particular, how can I increase the opportunities for peer and self-assessment, ipsative assessment and computer-assisted assessment?	

What results from assessment?		
	How can I broaden the range of assessment data that I collect in my teaching?	
	How do the data that I collect relate to: • my students' ability? • my planning, specifically the defined learning objectives for each lesson and unit of work? • National Curriculum or GCSE assessment frameworks?	
	How do my collected data help me plan for future learning effectively?	
	What is the correct balance between the quantity and quality of the assessment data I collect in my subject? Can less data produce a greater quality of outcome?	

What will you do after assessment?		
	How can I improve the storage of my assessment data using electronic or paper-based systems?	
	What changes can I make to the ways in which I interpret and analyse my assessment data to ensure that I utilise them in the most effective way?	

What will the student(s) do after assessment?		
	How do I build in opportunities for the sharing of findings drawn from assessment data with my students?	
	Do my strategies for assessment allow my students to construct a clear sense of progression for their learning within my subject? If not, how can I improve the systems or practices by which this could happen?	
	How do the outcomes of my assessment work feed into reporting practices to parents or the wider demands made on me for assessment data by senior managers within the school?	

Index

Added to a page number 'f' denotes a figure and 't' denotes a table.